EDITED BY DAVID S. KOETJE
FOREWORD BY RONALD J. SIDER

LIVING
THE GOOD LIFE

ON GOD'S GOOD EARTH

3.5 million Bushels –

D1369889

FAITH
ALIVE
Christian Resources

Grand Rapids, Michigan

Cover Photo: David S. Koetje

This book is one element of a project that developed out of a July 2003 workshop entitled "Christian Environmentalism With/out Boundaries" sponsored by Seminars in Christian Scholarship (SCS) at Calvin College, Grand Rapids, Michigan. The authors of this book are grateful for this SCS support and for additional funding from the Council for Christian Colleges and Universities via an Initiative Grants to Network Christian Scholars project, "Living as Part of God's Good Earth." To express this gratitude, the authors' stipends for this book were donated to the following exemplary Christian environmental organizations:

Creation Care Study Program (http://www.creationcsp.org)

A Rocha Canada (http://en.arocha.org/canada)

We welcome your comments. Call us at 1-800-333-8300 or e-mail us at editors@faithaliveresources.org.

Library of Congress Cataloging-in-Publication Data
Living the good life on God's good earth / edited by David S. Koetje.
    p. c.m.
   Includes bibliographical references.
   ISBN 1-59255-292-7
   1. Human ecology—Religious aspects—Christianity. 2. Nature—Religious aspects—Christianity. I. Koetje, David S., 1963-
   BT695.5.L58 2006
   261.8'—dc22
   2005036151

10 9 8 7 6 5 4 3 2 1

Chapter authors (listed alphabetically):

Mark D. Bjelland, Associate Professor of Geography, Gustavus Adolphus College, St. Peter, Minnesota

Steven C. Bouma-Prediger, John H. & Jeanne M. Jacobsen Professor of Religion, Hope College, Holland, Michigan

Susan P. Bratton, Professor and Chair of Environmental Studies, Baylor University, Waco, Texas

David R. Clements, Assistant Professor of Biology, Trinity Western University, Langley, British Columbia

Janel M. Curry, Dean for Research and Scholarship, Calvin College, Grand Rapids, Michigan

Lorynn R. Divita, Assistant Professor of Family & Consumer Sciences, Baylor University, Waco, Texas

Paul Heintzman, Assistant Professor of Human Kinetics, University of Ottawa, Ottawa, Ontario

David S. Koetje, Associate Professor of Biology, Calvin College, Grand Rapids, Michigan

Kenneth Piers, Professor of Chemistry and Biochemistry, Calvin College, Grand Rapids, Michigan

Bret Stephenson, Assistant Professor of Environmental Studies, Baylor University, Waco, Texas

David P. Warners, Associate Professor of Biology, Calvin College, Grand Rapids, Michigan

John R. Wood, Professor of Biology and Environmental Studies, King's University College, Edmonton, Alberta

Contributing Author:

Christiana de Groot, Professor of Religion and Chair of Gender Studies, Calvin College, Grand Rapids, Michigan

CONTENTS

FOREWORD

What were they thinking? Why would a team of Christian scholars collaborate on a book that dares to gives practical advice on what we should eat, what clothes we should wear, and even what kind of house we should live in? As Christians shouldn't they concern themselves with matters of the heart and the soul and leave the gardening tips to daytime television? And shouldn't they be more engaged with matters of the mind than how we spend our down time?

To be sure, there is a real danger that Christians forget or ignore their calling to spread the good news about Jesus worldwide. We can easily be distracted by falling back into the petty legalism that Jesus warned against, "Woe to you, teachers of the law and Pharisees, you hypocrites! You give a tenth of your spices . . . But you have neglected the more important matters of the law—justice, mercy and faithfulness . . . you strain out a gnat but swallow a camel" (Matt. 23:23-24).

In fact, the gospel that we are to bring to the world embraces all of life. It not only calls sinners to receive Jesus as their Savior, it also calls them to acknowledge him as Lord of all creation. Jesus announced: "All authority in heaven and on earth has been given to me. Therefore go and make disciples of all nations, baptizing them in the name of the Father and of the Son and of the Holy Spirit, *and teaching them to obey everything I have commanded you"* (Matt. 28:18-20).

Jesus has much to teach us about the way forgiven sinners treat the poor and the oppressed (Matt. 5:3-12). Jesus has much to teach us about the way we are to seek and to sacrifice for a Kingdom that is yet to come in fullness but that is already among us. Jesus has much to teach us about living as seasoning salt and as light in this present dark world (Matt. 5:13-14).

This book shows the fruit of deep and careful reflection on what Jesus' call to discipleship really means for the way we live our everyday lives on God's good earth. Despite the distortions caused by sin, this world is still God's handiwork. It still carries God's own promise that "the creation itself will be liberated from its bondage to decay and brought into the glorious freedom of the children of God" (Rom. 8: 21).

7

Paying careful attention to living the good life on God's good earth is not an abandonment of our Christian duty. And it is not a fallback into petty legalism. It is our labor of love

- for those who are in need,
- for those who will come after us should Jesus tarry,
- for the planet itself,
- and for the One who loves all these so much he died and now lives for them.

Surely this is an important, urgent topic for careful investigation by Christian scholars.

—Ronald J. Sider
President and Founder
Evangelicals for Social Action

1

CHRISTIAN THEOLOGY AND CREATION CARE

STEVEN C. BOUMA-PREDIGER AND BRET STEPHENSON

Susan Emmerich found herself in the middle of a mess. The year was 1998. Susan was living among a fishing community called the Tangier watermen and doing research for her doctoral degree on Tangier Island in the middle of the Chesapeake Bay. So far, so good. The problem was that pollution, disease, and over-harvesting had taken their toll, and there was only one fishery left—the blue crab. As a result, the people of Tangier Island were being pressured by a group of environmentalists, the Chesapeake Bay Foundation (CBF), to change their fishing habits. The watermen, meanwhile, had their own worries. They worried about their ability to put food on the table, and they worried about intrusion of outsiders into their way of life.

On both sides, tempers flared and emotions ran high. Some of the Chesapeake Bay Foundation folks were condescending toward the people of Tangier Island. Feeling powerless to reverse the decline of their fishery, the watermen, in turn, showed little respect for the environmentalist "outsiders" who used the abstract language of environmental science, who were clueless on matters of faith, and whose actions might seriously affect their livelihood. They were suspicious of the CBF, and for good reason. The impasse seemed insurmountable.

Like the Chesapeake Bay Foundation, Susan was anxious for the watermen to become better caretakers of their environment, but she took a very

9

different approach. Susan immersed herself in the island culture. She lived at the same economic level as the majority of the islanders. She dressed according to the island's conservative standards. She attended worship services and taught Sunday school at the local Methodist church. She helped the women process crabs. In all these ways, Susan showed her respect for the islanders' way of life. Her genuine care won the trust and garnered the love of many of the island people.

But it wasn't all a piece of cake. Susan was ostracized by certain members of the island community. She even received death threats. The process of influencing the community to better care for their marine resources was fraught with difficulties and required a lot of determination from Susan and from the islanders themselves as they began to discern the Spirit's beckoning.

FAITH-BASED STEWARDSHIP

In the end, a faith-based stewardship initiative, launched by Susan and led by the people of Tangier Island, yielded a cleaner island and a healthier fishery. Realizing that all sides desired a healthy Chesapeake Bay fishery, Susan helped the environmentalists at the Chesapeake Bay Foundation appreciate the watermen's faith-based cultural values. Likewise, she helped the watermen more fully live out the biblical faith they professed.

What caused Susan Emmerich's success on Tangier Island? No doubt her unique combination of communication skills, personal integrity, and uncommon wisdom had something to do with it. But more important, Susan tapped into a biblical ethic of stewardship that the watermen already possessed. This ethic is squarely rooted in a biblical theology common to all Christians and central to the Christian faith. It is a way of being in the world that acknowledges God as creator and sustainer of all things (Gen. 1-2), that understands God's covenant to be with all creation (Gen. 6-9), that stands in wonder at the symphony that is creation (Ps. 104), that acclaims Christ as the One in whom and for whom the whole creation hangs together (Col. 1), and that proclaims the glorious vision not of the annihilation of creation but of God's redemption of all things (Rev. 21-22).

In short, the biblical ethic embraced by Susan and the Tangier watermen is rooted in a theology of the greatness of God and the goodness of the earth. It implies that discipleship is learning to live the truly good life on God's good earth. That this theology and this ethic are not more widely embraced by Christians who cherish the Bible is one of the central scandals of our time.

A CALL TO DISCIPLESHIP

In this book we intend to show that Christian faith is not anti-ecological. Put more positively, we aim to illustrate how caring for the earth is integral to authentic Christian faith. And we aim to give plenty of practical guidance for living a life of ecological obedience and gratitude to God.

From where we live to what we eat, from how we use energy to what we grow in our yards, from what we do for work to how we spend our leisure time—in all these ways and more we are called as Christians to live our faith in our everyday life. Our goal is to provoke thought and provide insight, to empower action and foster hope, to challenge you to take seriously the call to discipleship in all you do.

What are the basics of the biblical theology common to Christians and central to the Christian faith? It starts with God, with the amazing conviction that God is a community of love—one God in three persons. And we know this God who is Love preeminently in the life, death, and resurrection of Jesus Christ. The homemaking God of Genesis 1-2 pitches his tent among us (John 1:14) and takes on human flesh to redeem and transfigure our bent and broken world.

This God creates all things (Gen. 1) and covenants with the earth and its plethora of creatures (Gen. 6-9). Creation is not necessary but it is natural. It is fitting that a relational God would enter into relationship with creation. So while God is distinct from creation, God is also in intimate relation to creation, lovingly upholding and sustaining all things (Ps. 104). All things are what they are by virtue of their relation to God and to other existing things. And all things—the birches and the bears, the marmots and the meadows—respond to God in their own creaturely ways (Ps. 148).

We humans are earthly creatures made in God's image. In other words, we are both Spirit-enlivened dirt (Gen. 2:7) and called to represent God and rule as God rules (Gen. 1:26-28): with concern for the common good, with care for the most vulnerable, with justice and compassion (Ps. 72). Our unique calling to this task of bearing God's image implies not just dominion but also service. We are earthly creatures called to serve the earth (Gen. 2:15).

In speaking of who we are, we need to emphasize that we live in relationship to God, to other humans, and to the nonhuman world. Created by God, we humans are dependent on God and made to be in loving relationship with the God who is Love. Indeed, our hearts are restless until they find rest in God (St. Augustine). But we are also created to exist among and live in communion with other humans (Gen. 2:18). We are social creatures. Our humanity is co-humanity. Furthermore, we humans are made from the dust of the earth—`âdâm from the `adâmâh (Gen. 2:7). We are dependent upon the earth—its nonhuman creatures, processes, and systems. So we are inextricably bound up not only with God and not only with other humans, but also with animals and plants, microbes and moles, the carbon cycle, symbiosis, and evapotranspiration.

We humans are not only related to other humans, we are embedded in a culture. We mature within certain family structures and learn certain languages. We inherit certain legal codes and assume certain economic practices. We take in not only certain kinds of food and drink but also certain artistic conventions and social customs. And we are embedded in particular places. We live immersed in distinct locales, we inhabit specific landscapes, and these places shape who we are, often in ways we do not realize.

NOT THE WAY IT'S SUPPOSED TO BE

This world of wonders made by God is, however, not the way it's supposed to be. It is bent and broken, warped and off-kilter (Gen. 3). Because of human disobedience, lack of trust, and pride, all creation does not yet sing God's praises undaunted, or delight in shalom. We are estranged from God, from each other, from our true best selves, and from the earth. Alienation stalks our every breath. The weight of inherited sorrow hangs on us like a sad song (Rom. 8).

And so God in Christ became flesh to redeem and to transfigure us and all creation. To do what we could not do by ourselves, God took on human form and made redemption possible. In Jesus, God defeats the powers of evil and we gain victory over sin and death (1 Cor. 15:57). In Jesus our bad debts are forgiven, and we are adopted into a new family (Rom. 4:25; Eph. 1:5). In Jesus our hurts are healed and we are reconciled with our enemies (2 Cor. 5:19). In Jesus we are ransomed from our captivity to self and liberated from the bondage of sin (Mark 10:45). In Jesus we are healed of our infirmities (Luke 7:22). In the life, death, and resurrection of our Messiah Jesus, the carpenter-rabbi from Nazareth, we see what God is really like, we learn of God's great love, and we attain life eternal.

The disciple John announces that this self-same Jesus, the Word, was "with God in the beginning" and "through him all things were made" (John 1:2-3). The apostle Paul says this same Jesus, the Lord of the cosmos, is the One in whom all creation coheres (Col. 1:17). This same Jesus, the Lion who is the Lamb, makes all things new (Rev. 21). And this same Jesus, the ruler and reconciler of all things, is the One for whom we hope and for whose reign of shalom we yearn.

This much, at least, is clear: the Christian faith, rooted in Scripture, provides more than ample reason to care for the earth. Indeed, as the Tangier watermen learned, caring for creation is an integral dimension of Christian discipleship. Earth care is part and parcel of what it means to be Christian! At stake is nothing less than the loving care of the earth and its creatures, a proper understanding of God, and the integrity of our faith itself.

In the chapters that follow we attempt to flesh out this life of discipleship, this living the good life on God's good earth. Rightly understood, it is a life of freedom and of joy, a life in which all things flourish as God intends— a life of shalom.

FOR REFLECTION AND DISCUSSION

1. What opportunities do you have to be a mediator and reconciler in the places where you live and work? How can you encourage people to work toward economic sustainability, social harmony, and ecological health?

2. If all things exist within the context of their relationships, which relationships are most difficult for you? Which ones give you joy? How do the things we buy relate us to other people and places? Does this have any moral significance?

3. How did Jesus rule? What does that mean for how we rule?

4. We can think of redemption in different ways: as God's gift of salvation for individual believers; as the gathering of a redeemed people, the church; or as God's work in Christ to redeem the whole of creation. Which of these resonates most with you? Why?

5. Why don't more Christians acknowledge that care for creation is integral to their faith? What obstacles prevent people from seeing Christianity as a religion that values the earth?

FOR FURTHER READING

Bouma-Prediger, Steven. *For the Beauty of the Earth: A Christian Vision for Creation Care*. Baker Academic, 2001.

DeWitt, Calvin. *Earth-Wise: A Biblical Response to Environmental Issues*. Faith Alive Christian Resources, 1994.

Hoezee, Scott. *Remember Creation: God's World of Wonder and Delight*. Eerdmans, 1998.

Quinn, Frederick. *To Heal the Earth: A Theology of Ecology*. Upper Room Books, 1994.

Sittler, Joseph. *Evocations of Grace: Writings on Ecology, Theology, and Ethics*. ed. Steven Bouma-Prediger and Peter Bakken. Eerdmans, 2000.

Wilkinson, Loren, and Mary Ruth Wilkinson. *Caring for Creation in Your Own Backyard*. Regent College, 1997.

RECOMMENDED DVD/VIDEO RESOURCE

Pohorski, Jeffrey. *Between Heaven and Earth: The Plight of the Chesapeake Watermen*. Skunkfilms Inc., 2001.

This Telly Award-winning documentary retells how Susan Emmerich recognized that the long-standing conflict between the watermen and the Chesapeake Bay Foundation revolved around the watermen's faith perspectives and how her faith-based stewardship perspective helped to resolve the conflict. 30 minutes. Available from Skunkfilms (www.skunkfilms.com).

THE WAY
WE LIVE

DAVID P. WARNERS AND SUSAN P. BRATTON

You've seen the signs: Adopt-a-Highway, Adopt-a-Stream, Adopt-a-Beach. Several times each year groups of volunteers sponsored by local companies, clubs, and civic organizations assemble to comb roadsides, riverbanks, and beaches for litter. Most of the time, they wind up collecting tons of debris: discarded food wrappers, cigarette butts, bottles, clothing, and unsavory rubbish tossed by careless souls or blown helter-skelter out of trash bins. Together these programs save taxpayers millions of dollars annually. In return, the sponsoring company or group is identified on signs for all to see and appreciate. One can only imagine what our landscapes would look like without these dedicated folks.

Generations ago, it was acceptable to throw trash away "out back" or into a nearby stream that could carry it away as flotsam. But as cities became crowded with people, we learned that throwing trash "away" often carried it to someone else's backyard! Not only that, but some of this trash was downright hazardous to people and to wildlife. Clearly something had to be done. To this end, sanitary landfills were invented. Problem solved. End of story, right?

Not exactly. Now we have a new problem. Landfills are rapidly filling up. Plans for new ones usually fall victim to the NIMBY ("not in my back yard") syndrome. Concerns about hazardous waste escalate as more high-tech devices are discarded. And so today it's not unusual to find municipalities hauling trash hundreds of miles across state and international borders. In fact, trash has become a major form of interstate commerce. Municipal recycling programs have helped to put a dent in the trash flow, but they still account for only a small fraction of our waste stream, which continues to grow. Isn't there a better solution?

A GROANING CREATION

North Americans consume a disproportionate amount of the planet's resources and produce a disproportionate amount of the planet's waste. While these are distinctions of our entire society, societies are made up of individuals who decide on a daily basis how to lead their lives. Do our lifestyles testify to our love for the Creator who gave his only Son out of deep love for the whole creation (John 3:16)?

Although humans alone were created in God's image, like God's other creatures we *homo sapiens* are enmeshed within God's handiwork; we interact with and affect the rest of creation. So when our activities require an unbalanced and significant sacrifice by the rest of creation, we need to ask whether our activities fit within a biblical framework of stewardship.

There is little doubt that the current impact of human beings on our land and on our fellow creatures is seriously jeopardizing the ability of the broader creation to flourish as God intended (Gen. 1:22). Consider, for instance, that the current rate of extinction is conservatively estimated at six to ten species *per day*—a rate far higher than in any other time in history, including the mass extinction period that led to the demise of the dinosaurs. The most troubling aspect of these numbers is that the primary cause of extinctions today is habitat loss exacted by human activities.

Species loss is one of many evidences that creation is groaning loudly. Others include global climate change, deteriorating quality of rivers and lakes, a decline in the global fishery industry, toxic contamination, and the ecological disruption caused by non-native species. Helping God to care for creation is a significant human responsibility, one that is neither optional nor avoidable (Gen. 1:26; 2:15). The lifestyle choices we make are a wonderful opportunity to show our commitment to stewardship and our love for God. What might such lifestyle choices look like?

RETHINKING FREE-MARKET CAPITALISM

Many North Americans live with the impression that our economic system (free-market capitalism) affords them a quality of life unparalleled on the global stage. After all, we have access to material goods, medical care, vacation opportunities, and other benefits that are beyond the means of most global inhabitants. Yet this quality of life is tarnished by numerous problems we often overlook: our disproportionate contribution to global climate change, toxic contamination and associated risk of cancer, significant loss of topsoil, drug abuse, crime, broken families, unprecedented teenage suicide rates, loneliness, depression, and obesity.

While many elements of North American culture are the envy of other countries, we would be wise to acknowledge that other cultures have some things worked out much better than we do. For example, contentment is typically not a hallmark that identifies North Americans. We are constantly led by our capitalist economic system to feel that we don't have enough. We feel we need to work harder, make more money, purchase more things, and look "better" in our continued pursuit of the always-evasive "good life."

The type of capitalism promoted in North America today is unilaterally profit- and growth-driven and is based on the fallacy of unlimited resources. It disregards the effects our actions have on the creation. At its core, this economic system is unsustainable. The challenge before us is to embrace capitalism's good contributions to life while identifying and avoiding the aspects that do not contribute to overall shalom in the creation.

In one such critical assessment, Bob Goudzwaard, a Christian economist from the Netherlands, calls for a conversion from a profit-driven economy to an economy of care and sufficiency. He suggests that businesses first use their profits to improve the lives of their workers and enhance the environmental and social well-being of their community before reinvesting them in the business itself. Herman Daly, former senior economist in the environmental department of the World Bank, similarly encourages an economy that is environmentally sustainable. He advises that we stop counting the consumption of natural capital as income, that we tax labor and income less while taxing resource depletion more, and that we support the development of local markets.

These new visions of capitalism recognize what is largely absent today: that all economic systems operate within the limits of the creation instead of beyond them. This type of thinking raises the very important question of sustainability—how long and to what extent can the lifestyles we enjoy be supported by a healthy, flourishing creation?

1. China used to tax food sold in local markets. When stopped doing this, came very close to feeding itself.

19

In his most recent book, *Collapse—How Societies Choose to Fail or Succeed,* Pulitzer Prize-winning author Jared Diamond examines what led great civilizations to collapse or flourish. He developed these criteria for assessing the long-term success of a culture:

- the nature of its relationships with neighboring societies,
- the degree to which it lives within the limits of its environmental context,
- the ways in which it contributes to and responds to climate change.

We can distill Diamond's criteria to a single question: How do our actions affect God's overall vision of shalom for the creation? When shalom (rather than profit or accumulation) is the guiding principle, human beings will live sustainably and at peace with the creation. As responsible and accountable stewards of God's good earth, such a vision should be at the heart of all our decisions.

A CHRISTIAN ENVIRONMENTAL ETHIC

Some environmentalists critical of Christianity contend that the Bible encourages a human-centered (or anthropocentric) approach to the environment. They claim that Christianity is environmentally inadequate because the Christian God is transcendent or external to the physical universe. Critics also accuse Christianity of teaching a self-centered form of dominion over the earth, where humans exploit the earth's resources.

In truth, Christianity has a rich tradition of environmental ethics and teachings on which we can draw. As we saw already in chapter 1, the triune God is not only transcendent but is immanent in the creation. God takes delight in the whale, the lion, and the stork in the cedars. The original Hebrew text of Genesis 2 implies that the Creator called on Adam and Eve not just to till the Garden but to *serve* Eden and to *preserve* it. Genesis 1:26, which calls for dominion, also implies that humans are servants of God, accountable as stewards to care for God's creation. And Noah's obedience to God in building an ark is a model of how God expects us to value other species. The Bible repeatedly testifies to God's love—not just for humans, but for the entire cosmos, which will be redeemed (see Rom. 8:21; Col. 1:19-20).

Christian environmental ethics is not simply about caring for nature; it also considers the needs of people who live within the creation. Psalm 104 offers a beautiful vision of shalom—a picture of how all of creation is intended to exist together. Human beings are clearly part of this picture. That leads us to ask how we can actualize such a vision of love and care in our daily lives.

We begin with the understanding that creation is more than God's gift to human beings to use as we please. Instead, it is a masterpiece created by a

God who loves every sparrow, delights in every monkey, and calls every human child to rest in his arms. We can reflect a Christian environmental ethic through four major forms of engagement in our daily lives. These are

- pursuing environmentally conscious lifestyles;
- caring for our home, regional, and global environments;
- caring for other species and for the earth's ecosystems; and
- restoring and healing degraded environments.

Of these, environmentally conscious lifestyles might seem the least important, but our lifestyles express who we are as Christians. The way we live our lives is essentially an activity of worship—our response of gratitude to the Creator. Discipleship must be lived with great care and compassion toward our fellow creatures.

EVERYDAY CHOICES

In our industrial economy, every item we wear, drive, sit on, eat, or watch was made by someone, shipped from somewhere, and eventually will be disposed of somehow. Since manufacturing is now a global venture, energy is usually invested in transporting raw materials long distances to processing points, and then transporting the finished goods even longer distances to consumers. Unlike our farming ancestors, who had a personal investment in the horses they raised, the cloth they wove, and the corn they ground, we moderns tend to see our daily necessities as lines of cardboard boxes and cars on the lot. In so doing we lose sight of the labor invested, the trees cut, and the land care involved in producing them.

A useful concept is the ecological cycle of energy and matter, which can be applied to our personal consumption of energy and materials. As a practical example, let's compare three types of tablewares: an ordinary ceramic plate and cup, a paper plate and cup, and a disposable plastic or Styrofoam plate and cup.

The material for the ceramic dishes came from a clay pit and is a non-renewable resource (although world stocks of clay can last many centuries). The clay is fired and glazed, then shipped to the consumer via truck or rail—all of which require energy. The ceramic plate and cup can be reused, and may even last decades before they are disposed of. Broken china is relatively inert and is not a major source of pollution, nor is it a major component of today's landfills.

The paper plate and cup are made from wood, which requires timber harvest that reduces forest cover and creates a direct impact on wildlife. Wood is a renewable resource, however, and logged forests can be reforested.

Paper manufacturing is a source of water pollution, and paper dishes must be thrown away after one meal. Because they cannot be recycled once used, paper plates and cups end up in incinerators or landfills. Those that are improperly disposed in a stream or in the forest adjoining a picnic area will, however, decompose in few years.

The plastic or Styrofoam plates and cups are made from petroleum products, requiring the international shipment of crude oil. North American dependence on non-domestic petroleum has sweeping social consequences, including drawing us into the tangled politics of the Middle East. Although these plates and cups could be washed and reused, most often they end up in the trash, where they tend to retain their form and take up large amounts of landfill space per unit weight. Improperly disposed of, plastic and Styrofoam dishes decompose slowly, persisting in the environment for many decades and posing a hazard to wildlife. Both the disposable paper and plastic table settings, with their short useful life spans, require more packaging and more energy for repeated shipping and hauling as waste.

In a family with a three-year-old child, dishwasher-safe plastic may be the most sensible tableware. But the comparison illustrates that a decision made at a Fourth of July picnic can have a significant environmental impact. And it raises questions that deserve our thoughtful response: How much petroleum should we buy internationally? How can we best share energy resources? How long do we want our landfills to last, and how much land are we willing to commit to disposable products that could be replaced by longer lasting counterparts? These questions are even more significant for larger and higher use products and services like automobiles and household water.

As Christians, we're called to wrestle with these everyday choices, big and small. In the words of Wendell Berry, "How we take our lives from this world, how we work, what work we do, how well we use the materials we use, and what we do with them after we have used them—all these are questions of the highest and gravest religious significance. In answering them, we practice, or do not practice, our religion" (*Sex, Economy, Freedom and Community*, 1992).

FOR REFLECTION AND DISCUSSION

1. How is "the good life" defined in North America? Who do you envision as having attained the good life? Is this consistent with the biblical vision of a good life? What are some aspects of your own life that, if changed, would draw you closer to achieving a good life?

2. Human beings are clearly distinct within the creation as the only creatures who bear God's image. Does an emphasis on our having been created "apart from" the rest of creation detract from our having been created "a part of" the rest of creation? Explain.

3. On a per capita basis, North American consumption far outdistances that of other cultures (we consume at least twice as much as Europeans). Why should this concern us?

4. In what ways can intentional behavioral choices for creation care show love for our neighbors? (Consider both space and time as you develop an answer to this question.)

5. If shalom were used as a criteria for our North American lifestyles, what difference would this make in North America? In your own life?

FOR FURTHER READING

Basney, Lionel. *An Earth-Careful Way of Life: Christian Stewardship and the Environmental Crisis.* InterVarsity Press, 1994.

Berry, Wendell. *Sex, Economy, Freedom and Community.* Pantheon, 1994.

Brown, Lester. *Eco-Economy: Building an Economy for the Earth.* W.W. Norton & Company, 2001.

Daly, Herman E., and Joshua Farley. *Ecological Economics: Principles and Applications.* Island Press, 2003.

Diamond, Jared. *Collapse—How Societies Choose to Fail or Succeed.* Penguin Group, 2004.

Goudzwaard, Bob, and Harry de Lange. *Beyond Poverty and Affluence: Toward an Economy of Care.* Eerdmans, 1995.

RECOMMENDED WEBSITES

- Creation Care Study Program: www.creationcsp.org. The Creation Care Study Program provides opportunities for Christian college students to study for a semester in Belize or the South Pacific (New Zealand and Samoa). Their academic program "connects Christian faith with the most urgent, complex global issues of the coming decades" and instills a sense of wonder at God's majesty revealed in the creation.

- Restoring Eden—Christians for Environmental Stewardship: www.restoringeden.org. Restoring Eden is a faith-based initiative that seeks to promote creation care as foundational within the emerging church movement. Restoring Eden chapters are active at a number of Christian colleges and universities. They have a close working relationship with the Creation Care Study Program.

THE HOMES WE LIVE IN

MARK D. BJELLAND

What would your dream home look like? Where would it be located? Perhaps you'd want it tucked away in the woods overlooking a lake, or somewhere with a stunning city view. What architectural style would it be? A sprawling Prairie style inspired by Frank Lloyd Wright, or maybe something classical and grand—the kind of thing you'd see featured in *Architectural Digest*?

What sort of rooms and features would your dream home have? Professional landscaping? An in-ground pool? A rec room with built-in gym or home theater? Would it be color-coordinated, Martha Stewart-style, or have personalized bedrooms that reflect the character of each family member? How close would your dream house be to your neighbors? Would you expect to get to know them or expect them to leave you alone?

Taking a virtual tour of your dream home makes one thing abundantly clear: a house is more than mere shelter. It meets our needs and desires at many levels. In addition to providing shelter and security, a house connects us to a community where we may find friends and a church home, get involved in local causes, and feel a sense of belonging. For many North Americans, a house represents their largest financial asset, so that during housing booms it is difficult not to get caught up in the quest for speculative real estate gains. For others, a house is a means of self-expression—as evidenced by the explosion of magazines, television programs, and stores catering to our collective fascination with home improvement. And for those who have achieved a certain level of worldly success, a grand house can serve as a highly visible symbol of status.

HOUSING DECISIONS MATTER

For Christians, decisions about where to live and what kind of house to live in are part of our walk with Christ. Following Christ means changing the way we think about houses and neighborhoods. It means seeing where we live not so much as an investment strategy, a status symbol, or a ticket to upward mobility, but as an important element of our discipleship. Housing decisions matter. The housing decisions we make affect the health of our communities and affect the quality of the environment—God's creation.

In order to be faithful disciples as we make decisions about where to live and what sort of house to live in, we need to be aware of the cultural forces that influence our choices and the way those choices affect the health of God's creation. But most of all, we need a biblical view of where our homes fit into God's purposes for our lives.

The Psalms, Proverbs, and the parables of Jesus make frequent references to houses and buildings. Houses symbolize where our treasures lie and what sort of foundations we have built our lives on. While Jesus had no place to lay his head, the biblical commands to fill the earth (Gen. 1:28) and tend the garden (Gen. 2:15) imply that most of us are to live settled lives, rooted in the places where God has placed us. While we await our true home in the New Jerusalem, we are called to pursue shalom—a right relationship to God, to our neighbors, and to creation—in the earthly locations where God has placed us. In the words of Jeremiah to the exiles in Babylon, we are to "build houses and settle down; plant gardens and eat what they produce. . . . Also, seek the peace and prosperity [shalom] of the city to which I have carried you . . . (Jer. 29:5, 7).

Houses give structure to our lives so that we can live the biblical vision of the good life on God's good earth—developing long-term relationships, tending the garden of God's creation, cultivating its aesthetic delights, practicing hospitality, and seeking the shalom of our city. Hospitality is an expression of the redemption and loving reception we experience in Christ. Whether welcoming children into the world, giving shelter to the stranger, or hosting a home fellowship group, houses are for hospitality.

We must, however, be careful that our houses do not become idols. The Scriptures contain warnings to those who build houses and barns without considering their Maker (Ps. 127:1; Luke 12:15-21), or who would join house to house in an expression of greed (Isa. 5:8). Thinking of our home in terms of shalom and hospitality might change the way we see it. It might influence the way we care for our lawn and garden as we attempt to show hospitality to all of God's creation. And it might change the way we view a proposal to build affordable houses or a new transit line in our neighborhood—not as a threat to property values but as way of showing hospitality and pursuing shalom.

MOVING UP, MOVING ON

In addition to shaping our personal lives, our housing decisions affect the health of communities. In five years, nearly half of North Americans will have moved to a different house, often motivated by the promise of upward social mobility (U.S. Census Bureaus, *Geographical Mobility, 1995-2000,* 2003). Moving to a new city or to a new neighborhood becomes a means of getting ahead—"moving up" in status and income. Frequently the American Dream is tied up with the ideal of moving "up" to a spacious suburban house set on a sprawling lot, far away from signs of poverty or decay.

This frequent moving weakens our relationships as we change neighborhoods, schools, and churches. When played out across vast metropolitan areas, our cultural ideal of moving up creates tragic consequences. Our individual restlessness creates a restless urban landscape, as those with economic means continually move on to newer housing on the edge of the city, while older neighborhoods with poorer residents are left behind to decay. Fearing threats to their property values, wealthy suburbs use zoning rules to keep out affordable housing, to segregate apartments away from single-family houses and workplaces away from houses. Thus the sprawling suburbs so closely identified with the American Dream are highly segregated, consume vast quantities of land, and require near total dependency on the automobile. Kids in these suburban havens rarely walk to school; their parents spend much of their time stuck in traffic. The net result of all these housing decisions is far from the state of shalom that we are to seek for our communities.

Housing decisions matter to the health of God's creation. If we use emissions of greenhouse gases as a way of measuring the pollution or the ecological footprint we individuals create, then the two most important factors in the size of our personal ecological footprint are the energy we use to heat, cool, and power our houses and the amount of gasoline we use in driving (U.S. Environmental Protection Agency, 2005).

Decisions about where to live and what sort of house to live in have a major influence on both of these factors. Consider size: as households have gotten smaller and smaller, our houses have gotten larger and larger, so that we now have about three times as much space per person as we did half a century ago. Larger houses translate into greater strain on creation as more land is consumed, more materials are used in construction, and more pollution is produced in the process of heating and cooling. While houses can be designed to significantly reduce energy costs and pollution, most of us are more concerned about kitchen layout or garage size than the effects of our house on God's creation.

Where we decide to live also has a major effect on the health of creation. For example, the average resident of sprawling, automobile-dependent cities such as Phoenix or Houston consumes twice as much gasoline (and therefore pollutes twice as much) as residents of the more compact city of Toronto where more people walk, bicycle, and use public transit. Per-person gasoline consumption in places like Phoenix and Houston is four to seven times that in prosperous Western European cities where walking, biking, and public transit are all popular (W. G. Newman and J.R. Kenworthy, "Gasoline Consumption and Cities," *Journal of the American Planning Association,* 1989, Vol. 55).

EFFORTS TO REGAIN COMMUNITY AND CREATION CARE

In the past, the Christian faith has expressed itself in the way that communities were built. For example, consider how the church served as the anchor and physical center of the community in the English village and the New England town. Today thoughtful Christians have raised the question of how, in our own social context, our discipleship might challenge us to move beyond cultural norms to reshape the places where we live. What follows is a brief description of efforts by various groups to regain community and creation care in housing.

New Urbanism

The New Urbanism movement in Canada and the United States is an attempt to recreate a sense of community, a strong place identity, and a more environmentally friendly way of living through improved urban design. New Urbanism calls for building traditional, compact, walkable, mixed-use communities—the kind that were built before World War II in the United States and Canada. Proponents of New Urbanism have developed many criteria for defining a good community, including the "popsicle test": Can an eight-year-old safely travel to the store for a popsicle by herself? Some research suggests that neighborhoods built according to New

Urbanist guidelines promote a strong sense of community and encourage residents to use transit and reduce their use of cars.

Conservation Communities

Conservation communities are appropriate for rural locations with large lot zoning. As it is typically employed, large lot zoning requires builders to have a minimum amount of land (such as 5, 10, or 40 acres) before they can build a house. Large lot zoning attempts to keep the rural "look" of a place and helps prevent the septic system of one house from contaminating a neighbor's well water. But scattering individual houses on 5- or 10-acre lots does not truly preserve the look or ecological value of the rural landscape. It also makes most agriculture impossible and requires excessive road construction.

Conservation communities, on the other hand, allow the same number of houses to be built but cluster them together into a village, creating a sense of community and preserving the remaining land for wildlife and agriculture.

Robert Engstrom, a long-time member of Hope Presbyterian Church in Richfield, Minnesota, runs a small family-owned development company. Engstrom pioneered the development of conservation communities in Minnesota. Engstrom's Fields of St. Croix development in Lake Elmo also pioneered the use of artificial wetland sewage treatment to allow houses to be clustered closely together. Most of the land is permanently preserved and held in common, including the lakeshore and a restored oak savanna. An existing farmstead was turned into an organic farm that supplies customers in the local community; a Civil War-era barn was converted into a community center. The Fields of St. Croix project was so popular that more than a dozen nearby projects have followed its approach.

Co-Housing*

In 2003 a small group of people met together to start a co-housing community in Grand Rapids, Michigan. In 2005, their vision began to fear fruit: Newberry Place will soon be under construction on an acre of land in the heart of the city. Fifteen households have committed themselves to alternative housing that values an urban location, diversity among its members, environmental responsibility, good design, and the promotion of community.

These values have translated into some very specific building decisions. The community will include households living in compact townhouses clus-

---

*Acknowledgment: Christiana deGroot contributed the piece on co-housing at Newberry Place. She looks forward to living as a member of that community.

tered around a common house. The common house provides space for the group to eat together several times a week, to socialize, and to build community. Although the common house is the central building on the site, parking is its most peripheral feature. Co-housing strives to keep much of the site green, usually including a children's playground and common garden. Respect for the environment results in a stewardly use of resources to heat and cool the buildings, taking advantage of natural ventilation, solar energy, and effective insulation. All of this is accomplished on a limited budget.

Although Newberry Place is not a Christian project per se, those of its members who are Christians see this housing alternative as a tangible expression of their call to be disciples. Its vision coheres with residents' convictions about the goodness of creation, the call to be reconciled to our neighbor, and a commitment to helping people flourish.

MAKING A DIFFERENCE IN YOUR LOCAL COMMUNITY

In many cities across the United States and Canada, living in a conservation community or a walkable community where one can walk to schools, churches, and local shops is not an option because such communities simply don't exist and can't be built under current zoning laws. In other cities, local zoning laws don't allow affordable housing, and local land use plans fail to protect wild places.

If that's true in your community, remember that local zoning laws and land use plans are a reflection of community interests. You and other Christians can decide to get involved in helping to make those local planning decisions. That kind of involvement is a form of the kind of stewardship we're called to as disciples of Christ. It's a way of seeking the shalom of the city where God has placed us.

FOR REFLECTION AND DISCUSSION

1. Describe your ideal place to live. What has shaped your ideals for houses and neighborhoods?

2. How does the biblical vision of living the good life on God's good earth differ from the American Dream? In what ways do you sense the Lord calling you to seek shalom in the place where you live?

3. What are the warning signs that a house has become an idol?

4. How might our attitudes, actions, and the look of our communities change if we were to view our house and our neighborhood as an important part of our walk with Christ, our ministry, and our stewardship of creation?

5. What are some steps you could take to reduce the size of your home's ecological footprint?

FOR FURTHER READING

Arendt, Randall, Elizabeth Brabec, Harry Dodson, Christine Reid, and Robert Yaro. *Rural by Design: Maintaining Small Town Character*. American Planning Association Press, 1994.

Bjelland, Mark D. *Thinking Regionally: Justice, Nature, and City Planning*. Crossroads Monograph Series on Faith and Public Policy, Evangelicals for Social Action, 1999.

Duany, Andres, Elizabeth Plater-Zyberk, and John Speck. *Suburban Nation: The Rise of Sprawl and the Decline of the American Dream*. North Point Press, 2001.

Gillham, Oliver, and Alex S. Maclean. *The Limitless City: A Primer on the Urban Sprawl Debate*. Island Press, 2002.

Jacobsen, Eric O. *Sidewalks in the Kingdom: New Urbanism and the Christian Faith*. Brazos Press, 2003.

THE FOOD
WE EAT

JANEL M. CURRY AND DAVID S. KOETJE

> To receive the gift of creation and then to hasten to practical ways of exploiting that gift for maximum production without regard to long-term impacts is at best ingratitude and at worst blasphemy (the act of claiming for oneself the attributes and rights of God).
>
> —Wendell Berry, from a letter read at the "Theology of Land" conference, 1986

Only when the cement was being poured did a small town in Michigan learn the identity of its new neighbor—a large corporate hog-production facility. Labor for the facility was imported from outside the community, along with feed and other products. Local tensions rose over environmental and community impacts. Endless meetings were held; some neighbors were no longer on speaking terms.

Unfortunately, this is not an isolated incident. Drive along any major highway throughout the Midwest and you'll see evidence that such conflicts are widespread. What's going on here?

Ask North Americans about their mental image of farming, and they're likely to conjure up something like the scene in Norman Rockwell's painting *The County Agricultural Agent:* an agricultural extension agent consults with a sturdy, proud farm family surrounded by an assortment of animals in front of a bright red barn. Idyllic and agrarian, the scene is prominently displayed in many agricultural extension offices. But it no longer reflects agriculture in North America. Our meat and poultry products are primarily raised in large-scale confined-animal feeding operations (CAFOs) such as feedlots of more than 15,000 cattle, or chicken houses of 25,000 birds. Fully half of all American cropland is devoted to just two species: corn and soybeans. Of that corn, less than 10 percent is consumed directly as food in the United States. The remainder is fed to livestock, exported, or used to produce fuel ethanol or high fructose corn syrup.

In the early twentieth century, laborers were needed in the growing manufacturing sector. Labor-saving machinery on farms allowed people to move to cities, where the middle class blossomed. As the trend continued, many who sincerely wanted to farm found that they could no longer afford to do so. Very large farms with sales over $500,000 (now 8 percent of the total in Canada and 4 percent in the United States) account for more than half of agricultural revenues, a share maintained through lucrative contracts with food wholesalers and retail conglomerates. Today the moderate-sized family farm is an endangered species, along with many of the rural towns whose economies are dependent on providing services to these farm families.

BIGGER DOESN'T ALWAYS MEAN BETTER

As farms grow in size, reliance on fertilizers, feeds, and energy increases. Instead of simply spreading manure on pastures to nourish plants to be eaten by livestock, CAFOs rely on processed feeds produced using fossil fuel-derived fertilizers, which are usually trucked in from hundreds of miles away. Crop rotations, once used to manage pests and diseases on farms, have been replaced by continual single cropping and chemical pesticides. In farming areas, local municipalities post seasonal warnings to discourage young children and pregnant women from drinking nitrate-laden water contaminated by nitrogen fertilizer.

This does not sound like an ecologically sustainable food system. It probably isn't economically sustainable either. Rising fuel prices affect the cost of producing and transporting food—by the time foods reach our grocery shelves, most have been trucked 1,500-2,000 miles from processing plants to centralized wholesale warehouses to retailers. Ultimately, our current farm system is not socially sustainable either. As farm size increases, small communities struggle to maintain the foundations of their existence: schools, churches, and businesses. Even organic farming is not immune to these size-related trends.

HOG PRODUCTION AND FAITH QUESTIONS

Let's look at one example, the expansion of hog CAFOs, to explore faith questions that underlie the choices and tensions involved in our farm systems and food production.

As recently as 1985, hog production still took place on thousands of small independent farms in the Midwest that produced a few hundred animals each year. In contrast, the CAFO system of production involves feeding thousands. Animals are put in individual pens that are so small the animal can't turn around. Strict access policies protect against the spread of disease among the genetically similar and concentrated group of hogs. Hogs produce four times as much waste as humans, so another CAFO feature is large manure lagoons. Mechanical systems collect waste and distribute feed. When the facility is not directly owned by a corporation, farmers are usually contracted. The company provides pigs, feed, and veterinary services; farmers provide land, buildings, labor, utilities, and management. The scale of the transformation of hog production in recent years is mind-boggling! One such corporately-owned hog farm in Utah has plans for a 100,000-sow operation capable of producing two million animals per year for the West Coast market.

So what are the biblical principles that can help us think about the issues surrounding the food we eat and how it is produced? As creatures made in the image of God, we are fundamentally relational beings. This relational nature finds expression not just in relations between human beings, but also between humans and the land (Gen. 2:15; Hos. 4:1-3). Also central to the relational aspect of creation is the biblical theme of a covenant between God and a people—a covenant that involves obligations to God and one's neighbor that transcend self-interest and promise a deep sense of self-fulfillment.

When we begin with this image of ourselves as relational beings, our food production choices appear less neutral. We may find that they are grounded in a view of humans as fundamentally autonomous individuals, each pursuing their own economic interests. Agricultural policies are only meant to facilitate individual advancement. Excluded from such policy discussions are community attachment, community vitality and richness, and environmental "fit."

So how do hog CAFOs measure up against the biblical principle of relatedness? Opponents are concerned that CAFOs violate the principle of relational wholeness because they fail to be embedded in earth's systems. For instance, hogs are produced in North Carolina with shipments of corn from the Midwest on a soil base that can neither absorb the manure being produced nor grow the corn needed for the hogs. That system has proven risky. Hurricanes in North Carolina were considered a minimal risk until 1999, when manure lagoons broke, spilling their contents across the coastal plain and into the Atlantic, creating a marine dead zone.

Such systems are disconnected from the human community as well. Contributing little to community life except a few farm labor jobs and perhaps sponsorship of a local softball team, CAFO corporations do not exhibit long-term commitment to any one place; rather, they move from state to state. In fact, they generate fewer economic benefits to the local economy than those obtained from smaller-scale independent hog farmers who buy from local suppliers. As a result, community economic health suffers.

GENETICALLY MODIFIED FOODS

Focusing on our relationality provides insights into many food production issues, including concerns about the use of biotechnology. Though sometimes touted as key to improving agricultural sustainability and food security, genetically modified foods are the focus of a global trade dispute centered on the United States and the European Union. Many trace the problem to different experiences with food safety, but the roots of the dispute are actually much deeper.

Local cuisines are a major part of Europeans' sense of place, and farms are key in their conservation efforts. In contrast, North American mobility prevents us from developing much of a sense of place, except for the tracts of "pristine" wilderness that we set aside as nature preserves. Thus, most North Americans have little regard for where our food comes from as long as it is safe.

Given these ideological differences, the dispute is understandable. North American governments use agricultural biotechnology to battle nature's barbs—pests, diseases, environmental fluctuations, and the like, to pioneer food innovations, and to increase food safety. European governments respond with precaution, concerned that biotechnologies, developed with little regard to place, may undermine Europeans' commitment to unique places, products, and communities. This difference in approach illustrates how our understanding of the interrelationships between humans and environments has profound implications for the types of agriculture we choose to develop and implement.

ALTERNATIVES

What hope is there for a more biblical vision of food production in North America? Can we find places where Christian discipleship is evident in our food systems? Alternatives do exist—alternatives that incorporate a more relational view of humans, nature, and God. These do not try to take us back to some Norman Rockwell vision of the "ideal" past, but rather point forward, using our developing scientific knowledge to move toward relational wholeness.

For an example of such an alternative, let's get back to those hogs. The "hoop system" is an economically competitive hog farming system in which the farmer continually adds bedding to the floor of hoop structures over a six-month period, creating heat from the composting of the pig manure and straw while creating a solid fertilizer to be spread on fields. The sows live on bedding in a group with feeding stalls, mimicking their natural setting. This system relies less on equipment, automation, and buildings to control pigs, and instead requires intensive husbandry—involving relationships with natural systems. Behavioral studies show that farmers and pigs seem to like the hoops. And so do their neighbors! Support for policies that recognize the fundamental need for wholesome relationships with God, with our communities, with animals, and with the land reflect one aspect of our Christian discipleship.

But Christian discipleship in matters of food also involves individual choice. Community-based agriculture is intended to empower both individuals and their communities. Its vision is to sustain small and mid-sized enterprises that build relationships with local consumers. It also emphasizes local knowledge that is sensitive to the "expectations of the land." Farmers raise crops and livestock in the context of local resources, and local people take pleasure in eating what is grown locally and in knowing about their food source. The economy of these "foodsheds" is shaped and expressed in communities attempting to build sustainable relationships among themselves and with the land.

Every time we buy locally and choose products in season from our local area, we are symbolically and concretely reflecting the wonderful relational nature of being made in God's image. And when our policies and individual choices match the realities of our relational nature, we are moving toward agricultural practices that reflect the Creator's desire for shalom.

FOR REFLECTION AND DISCUSSION

1. Compare your notions of farming and agriculture to the realities of CAFOs. What values are reflected in the transformation of agriculture exemplified by CAFOs?

2. What difference might a more intentional focus on our interrelatedness with God, with our neighbor, and with the land make in your purchasing choices? What options are available in your area to support local farmers and food businesses? How might churches support local farmers and local production?

3. What is the connection between our society's values and our attitudes toward genetically modified foods?

Not explained

4. The concept of a "foodshed" encompasses where our food comes from and how it gets to us. Take a quick inventory of the foods you buy. Where does this food originate? What crops are available locally and in what season? Where can you go to buy them?

5. In what ways do the principles that underlie the hoop system of hog production conform to Christian discipleship and environmental stewardship? How might these principles be applied to other aspects of food production in your area?

FOR FURTHER READING

Curry, Janel M. "Industrial Hog Farms vs. God's Desire for Shalom." *Creation Care: A Christian Environmental Quarterly* No.15 (Fall 2001): 12-13.

Evans, David J., Ronald J. Vos, and Keith P. Wright. *Biblical Holism and Agriculture: Cultivating our Roots*. William Carey, 2003.

Halweil, Brian. "Home Grown: The Case for Local Food in a Global Market." *Worldwatch Institute Paper #163* (2002); available at http://www.worldwatch.org/pubs/paper/163/.

Schreur, Edward Hart. "The Swine Crisis and the Church." *Perspectives: A Journal of Reformed Thought* 15 (2000): 3.

Jackson, Wes. *Altars of Unhewn Stone: Science and the Earth.* NorthPoint Press, 1987.

Schlosser, Eric. *Fast Food Nation: The Dark Side of the All-American Meal.* Houghton Mifflin, 2001.

5

THE CLOTHES WE WEAR

LORYNN R. DIVITA

There aren't any sweatshops in America! That's what many people thought, at least before August 2, 1995—the day police officers and the California Department of Industrial Relations raided an apartment complex in the Los Angeles suburb of El Monte.

There they discovered an apparel manufacturing sweatshop not unlike those in Thailand and Malaysia. Owned and run by a Chinese-Thai family, it employed seventy-two illegal Thai immigrants, mostly women. Fences surrounding the complex were covered in barbed wire to prevent escape. The owners had seized the workers' documentation papers. Inside, authorities found apparel for several American manufacturers and retailers, most of whom paid a $2.5 million settlement to workers without having to admit to any guilt in the violations. Each manufacturer claimed it was unaware of the illegal operation.

Local people were horrified to discover that this abuse had occurred right in their own community. But the fact that the same abhorrent conditions exist in many other countries seemed to escape them. Was the impact of these working conditions so much greater because of the sweatshop's proximity? Is the issue of sweatshops truly "out of sight, out of mind"?

They can't store corn in the Southern U.S. because insects (weevil) aren't killed by freezing.

Sweatshops have been around since the Industrial Revolution, and the textile and apparel industries have always relied heavily on women and children for labor. A century ago, poor working conditions in the apparel industry were tolerated in America. But things changed dramatically on March 25, 1911, when a fire broke out at the Triangle Shirtwaist Company in New York City, killing 146 workers. That disaster prompted legislation regulating working conditions, the number of hours in a workweek, and minimum wages (Gini Frings, *Fashion from Concept to Consumer*, 3rd ed., Prentice Hall).

ENVIRONMENTAL IMPACT

The textile industry has not only had a negative impact on society, but it has adversely affected the environment. The production of cotton, for example, involves the use of chemicals for fertilization, insecticides, growth control, and harvesting. In fact, commercial cotton growers use more than 275 million pounds of pesticides annually in the United States, which is 35 percent of total worldwide pesticide use (www.clothingmatters.net/education/cotton.html).

Heavy chemical use creates the possibility of contaminated wastewater. Cotton crops require at least 20 inches of rain per year, and if this amount cannot be achieved naturally, the land must be irrigated. Soil erosion from tilling also impacts the land. After the harvest, soil and natural waxes must be removed from the raw fibers, which are further processed by bleaching, dyeing, and the application of more chemicals to impart properties such as stain resistance. These processes require large quantities of heat, water, energy, chemicals, and solvents. In countries without environmental legislation, wastewater containing dye is often dumped into the same rivers that people fish in and get drinking water from. Even the stonewashing that gives jeans that gently worn look produces a pile of silt from broken-down stones. The silt is poured into lakes and rivers, affecting their plant life. Finally, scrap fabric is often dumped into a landfill, taking decades to decompose, instead of being recycled.

Environmentally friendly alternatives to commercially grown cotton exist in the form of organic cotton and hemp, but our consumption of these in North America is miniscule compared to that of commercially grown cotton. Organic cotton is expensive, but it is grown without any pesticides or herbicides, and can even be grown in colors, eliminating the need for dying. And hemp suffers from a stigma caused by consumers' confusing industrial hemp with the marijuana plant. (Interestingly, this association has not always existed—many Christian farm families grew hemp during World War II for rope manufacturers.)

CLOTHING AND TEXTILES IN THE BIBLE

The Bible doesn't talk about sweatshop labor or the damage our textile production inflicts on the environment. But it is filled with references to clothing and textiles that may help us make some sense of how what we wear fits into a life of Christian discipleship.

The symbolic imagery used in the Bible regarding clothing underscores its importance in everyday life. In Psalm 139, the psalmist describes the beginnings of his life by picturing God as a weaver and his mother's womb as a loom: "My frame was not hidden from you when I was made in the secret place. When I was woven together in the depths of the earth, your eyes saw my unformed body" (vv. 15-16a). Other biblical references to clothing illustrate the wearer's social status. For example, the parable of the rich man and Lazarus begins with a description of the young ruler's clothing: "There was a rich man who was dressed in purple and fine linen and lived in luxury every day" (Luke 16:19). God even told the Israelites to put distinctive tassels on their cloaks to signify that they were a people set apart (Deut. 22:12).

Some biblical references to clothing and textiles take on a deeper meaning by serving as metaphors for how we as Christians ought to live our lives. The Greek verb _enduo_ ("to put on"), which is frequently used in relation to clothing throughout the Bible, can have a double meaning. In addition to the literal meaning of wearing clothing, it can also refer to one's state of being, as in Paul's instruction "Therefore, as God's chosen people, holy and dearly loved, clothe yourselves with compassion, kindness, humility, gentleness and patience" (Col. 3:12).

What if we could clothe ourselves with compassion not just figuratively but literally? Companies that value human rights and environmental responsibility along with making a profit do exist. Adam Neiman, founder of No Sweat Apparel in Waltham, Massachusetts, says he initially started his company to prove a point: "I was not able to persuade my children that they had the ability to change the world. There wasn't really anything that would prove it to my kids unless I did it myself." No Sweat challenges larger companies to improve their own labor standards. "If we can do this on a shoestring, how much money would it take for Nike to do that? And if they don't know their contractors' wages and benefits, then how do they know that they've dealt with the sweatshop issue?" Neiman also has a reply to the claim that sweatshops are a "necessary evil" in the economic development of any nation. "You don't work to perpetrate a necessary evil. Take that as a starting point and go from there. I wouldn't want to be running a sweatshop, but if the next phase up is a unionized garment industry, I think I'd like to be a part of that."

Neiman sees his business venture as evidence of his faith. "If you're religious in this country, then you've got to believe in loving thy neighbor as thyself." He sees common goals with religious activists in China, which is home to some of the worst sweatshop conditions anywhere. "Human rights are a package deal. You don't get religious rights without labor rights." Neiman's philosophy has resulted in a company that sells its products online and in 135 stores around the world.

CLOTHING OURSELVES WITH COMPASSION

Even though we may not see the people in foreign countries (or our own!) who work in sweatshops and who deal with the environmental fallout of textile production on a daily basis, we are inextricably interrelated to them. That's because the work they do provides us with the clothes on our backs.

When Jesus told his disciples to take up their crosses and follow him, they knew they would have to make sacrifices. And if our discipleship today compels us to refuse to purchase clothing made with sweatshop labor or environmentally unsafe production methods, we can expect to make sacrifices too. What kind of sacrifices? Perhaps consuming less clothing, paying more for garments made with organically grown cotton, or not purchasing something we like because it is made in a country with known sweatshop problems. These are countercultural decisions. Clothing is such a basic part of our lives that we often fail to consider how it makes its way into our closets. At the same time, keeping companies that exploit their workers and the environment in business is an indictment of our Christian values. So what can we do?

Let's begin by asking the question "How does this issue affect my life?" and by changing the way we do things. Consider the suggestions in the chart on page 45, and commit to practicing them. After all, what could be a more fitting response to Paul's call to clothe ourselves in compassion and kindness?

Practical

What You Can Do	
Purchase fewer articles of clothing, but of better quality.	Consumers' appetites for cheap clothing have resulted in spending without moral or social accountability for what they purchase. This lack of accountability enables corporations and consumers to shirk their stewardship responsibilities.
Hold apparel manufacturers and retailers responsible for their actions.	Research companies' environmental and sweatshop histories on websites such as www.responsible shopper.org or the Retailer Report Card at http://www.coopamerica.org/programs/sweatshops/scorecard.cfm. If you hear about human rights or environmental infractions perpetrated by a particular company, let them know you won't be purchasing their products until they address this problem.
Recycle your unwanted textiles and apparel.	Donate them to a charity such as Goodwill for resale. Or, if your community has a recycling center that handles textiles, bring them there to be made into other products.

GMO - Genetic Modified

FOR REFLECTION AND DISCUSSION

1. What is our responsibility as consumers and end-users for the conditions under which our possessions are made?

2. Is the legal code a sufficient barometer of our values, or should Christian disciples have a different set of standards? How should we determine what these standards might be? For example, it may be legal to dump untreated wastewater into a river in some countries, but is it acceptable?

3. How are we related to communities on the other side of the planet, especially those that don't share our values?

4. What case can be made for purchasing decisions based on factors other than cost? As followers of Jesus, how can our choice of clothing be a sacrificial act?

5. What happens when two of our beliefs appear to be contradictory? For example, some people reject hemp products because of hemp's association with marijuana, but the environmental impact of commercially-grown cotton is far worse.

FOR FURTHER READING

Rosen, Ellen Israel. *Making Sweatshops: The Globalization of the U.S. Apparel Industry.* University of California Press, 2002.

Rivoli, Pietra. *The Travels of a T-shirt in the Global Economy.* John Wiley & Sons, 2005.

Yafa, Stephen. *Big Cotton: How a Humble Fiber Created Fortunes, Wrecked Civilizations, and Put America on the Map.* Viking Adult, 2004.

RECOMMENDED WEBSITES

- Clothing Matters (www.clothingmatters.net). Learn more about the benefits of hemp and organically grown cotton at this retailer's website.

- No Sweat Apparel (www.nosweatshop.com). Learn more about the company's social activism and purchase apparel and footwear made entirely at union facilities under sweatshop-free conditions.

- Smithsonian Institution (http://americanhistory.si.edu/sweatshops/index.htm). See an online exhibition about the El Monte sweatshop story at this website.

THE ENERGY
WE USE

KENNETH PIERS

The year is 2030. Olivia, a young woman in her early thirties, has just completed her work day. As an accountant for a large firm, Olivia uses electronic and wireless technology in her home office in suburban Chicago. The weather outside is hot and dry, as it has been for the past several months. Today the air conditioning in her tenth-floor apartment is working, but rolling blackouts of electrical service make this a luxury to be appreciated.

Olivia decides to do a little grocery shopping because the elevator is in service today. Yesterday she would have had to walk down from the tenth floor to get outdoors. She walks eight blocks to the grocery store because gasoline for her gasoline-electric hybrid vehicle is being rationed. A war in the Middle East that has persisted for more than five years has severely limited the output of crude oil. Not only is gasoline in short supply, it is also very costly—more than $7.00 per gallon. That means fresh vegetables, bread, and milk are all very pricey too, since the shortage of gasoline and natural gas from which to make fertilizer has also caused a drop in agricultural output. In fact, Olivia feels fortunate to find some fresh-baked bread on the shelves.

Because Chicago is on the shores of Lake Michigan, water is relatively abundant, though costly. Elsewhere, climate change and population pressure have caused water shortages in large urban centers such as Phoenix, Las

Vegas, and Los Angeles. Many people have left these cities in favor of regions with a more abundant and reliable supply of water.

These situations aren't short-term problems for Olivia. They're a way of life.

ENERGY AND MODERN CIVILIZATION

North Americans have become accustomed to a reliable and inexpensive supply of energy resources. When we wake up in the morning and turn on the light switch, we expect the room to light up. When we turn up the thermostat in our house, we expect the furnace to warm our house. When we turn the ignition key in our car we expect the motor to start.

But the electricity that powers the light bulb is probably produced in a coal-burning power plant located many miles from our house. Our furnaces are probably fueled by natural gas supplied via a vast network of underground pipelines originating in Wyoming or Alberta. The fuel that powers our cars is a product of crude oil that may have come from Texas, Saudi Arabia, Venezuela, northern Alaska, or from the tar sands of northern Alberta.

These everyday examples illustrate that modern civilization is utterly dependent upon fossil fuels such as coal, oil, and natural gas. Eighty-five percent of the energy we use is provided by these resources. Prior to about 1750, all civilizations had access only to renewable energy such as solar energy and its derivatives: wind, water, wood, animal, human, and so on. Today we characterize such societies as pre-modern.

The United States and Canada are huge energy consumers. Every day we use about 22 million barrels of oil (a barrel is equal to 42 U.S. gallons; about 160 liters), about 2 billion cubic meters of natural gas, and nearly 3 million tons (3 billion kg) of coal. Ninety-five percent of our transportation systems (car, truck, train, bus, airplane, boat) use oil-derived fuels. Our food production and distribution system is completely dependent on access to petroleum for fuel, for fertilizer, and for transport to markets. Modern urban, suburban, and rural civilization is inconceivable without the use of these fossil fuel energy inputs.

FOSSIL FUELS AND SUSTAINABILITY

So what's the problem? Petroleum industry analysts warn us that worldwide oil production is likely to reach a peak within the next ten or fifteen years, if not sooner, just as domestic U.S. oil production peaked 35 years ago. These predictions are based on oil production data, analysis of published "proven" oil reserve figures, and on oil discovery data. Oil discovery rates worldwide peaked in the early 1960s. Currently we are consuming oil about four times faster than we are discovering new oil.

It is essential for us to recognize that societies dependent on oil and natural gas—both of which are non-renewable in historic time—for about 65 percent of their primary energy supply are not sustainable without fundamental changes in their energy supply structure. In fact, such societies are in great danger of decline or even collapse, should these resources become less available. There are now significant indications that we are not far from the time when worldwide production of oil will reach a maximum. United States production of natural gas (currently still a regional rather than a global resource) is already showing signs of decline.

FOSSIL FUELS AND THE ENVIRONMENT

Besides supply issues, there are environmental reasons why our heavy reliance on fossil fuels is not sustainable. Global warming, urban smog, and acid rain all are directly attributable to our heavy and widespread use of fossil fuels. Every time we burn fossil fuels, whether coal, oil, or natural gas, exhaust gases are emitted (carbon dioxide, which is implicated in global warming; nitrogen oxides, which are involved in urban smog and acid rain; and, in the case of coal, sulfur oxides, which contribute to acid rain). These gases enter the atmosphere and are carried into the surrounding regions by wind and weather. There are increasingly clear signs that the atmosphere has a limited capacity to withstand all of the effluents that we discharge into it.

CONSERVATION STRATEGIES

If sustainability issues suggest that we need to curtail our use of fossil fuels, what options are available? The first strategy that comes to mind is energy conservation. Conservation has two main aspects. One option is to engage in fewer energy-intensive activities. A second option is to improve the efficiency of our energy use. The table below lists some specific conservation strategies.

Conservation by Lowering Demand	Conservation by Improving Efficiency
1. Raise your household thermostat a few degrees in the summer; lower it a few degrees in the winter. 2. Turn down thermostats at night and when not at home in winter; turn off air conditioning at night and use a window fan in the bedroom.	1. Improve efficiency of private transportation—choose high-efficiency diesel; gasoline-electric hybrids; diesel-electric hybrid; plug-in gasoline-electric; all-electric vehicles.

Conservation by Lowering Demand	Conservation by Improving Efficiency
3. Turn down the thermostat on your water heater a few degrees.	2. Use high efficiency lighting for your home: compact fluorescent, LED lighting.
4. Coordinate errand-running and shopping trips into a single event and plan the driving route to minimize travel distance.	3. Improve home insulation.
5. Travel during non-peak hours to minimize traffic jams on freeways.	4. When they wear out, replace old, energy-demanding appliances such as water heaters, refrigerators, furnaces, and air conditioners with high-efficiency appliances.
6. Use public transit when and where possible.	
7. Use trains for inter-urban travel when possible.	5. Schedule an energy audit for your home (many power companies provide this service).
8. Use a bicycle or walk when possible, and encourage local traffic policies that are bicycle- and pedestrian-friendly.	
9. Choose living arrangements that are close to one or more of the following: your place of work, your church, schools, or shopping areas.	6. Replace windows with more efficient windows.
	7. Seal leaks near your home's foundation, roofline, and doors.
10. Make energy demands part of your consideration when considering recreational or leisure activities.	8. Enhance inter-urban passenger train service.
11. Carpool with neighbors or work mates.	9. Reduce urban sprawl.
12. Use a manual push lawn mower.	10. Develop public mass transportation systems.

RENEWABLE ENERGY SOURCES AND SUSTAINABILITY

Ultimately, conservation is only one component of any energy policy (though it's a component that is low-cost and easily enacted). We also need to find energy sources that replace oil and natural gas, which is not easy. There is no primary energy source on the horizon that combines all the positive qualities of crude oil (abundant, relatively inexpensive to produce, easily shipped and stored, high energy density).

In the long term, it seems that a fully sustainable energy policy needs to be based on renewable resources. But the most obvious of these—wind and direct solar power—suffer the disadvantages of low energy density and sporadic availability. For example, to replacing the electrical energy generated by one 1,000 megawatt (MWe) coal-fired power plant operating 80 percent of the time, you'd need to construct about sixteen hundred 2 MWe wind turbines (assuming that these can operate at 25 percent capacity). The output from these turbines—electricity—cannot be easily stored on a large scale.

So reliance on wind or solar energy as primary electricity sources is limited by the need for a reliable back-up system for those times when the wind is not blowing and the sun is not shining. Such systems are now provided mainly by coal or natural gas-fired power plants or nuclear power plants. Hydroelectric energy plays a small role in the U.S. energy picture and a larger role in the Canadian energy supply. However, most of the best hydroelectric sources in these countries have already been developed.

Energy from plant materials (biomass) is a relatively non-polluting source of primary energy, depending on the biomass source. Currently the United States converts a substantial amount of corn into ethanol, which is used as fuel when blended with gasoline in the product gasohol. However, most objective studies of this process reveal that more fossil fuel energy is used in the planting, harvesting, shipping, and processing of the corn than is contained in the ethanol so produced. So, from the perspective of developing a sound energy policy, this is not a good practice.

Because biomass has a low energy density, a successful system for using biomass as a source of fuel requires that the plant source use very little fossil fuel energy in its production. One possible source that is perhaps more promising than corn is found in certain hardy perennial grasses, such as switch-grass. These grasses use relatively little fossil fuel energy and are highly productive. Although the production of liquid fuels from grasses is less straightforward than fermentation of corn to ethanol, several options appear promising. Here again, however, because of the low energy density of bio-based fuels, large acreages would need to be devoted to grass farming in order to make a substantial contribution to national fuel needs.

CONCLUSION

So what do we make of all this from a Christian perspective? Clearly, our society must transition to an energy system that is more sustainable than fossil fuels. Doing so is in keeping with the biblical call to justice, stewardship, and discipleship. But we must recognize that such a transition will itself require substantial inputs of energy. We're called, therefore, to adopt lifestyles that conserve limited fossil fuel resources for as long as possible. Such changes will challenge us as North Americans. Each person, family, and community will need to reflect creatively on ways to reduce our energy demands.

Thinking about the energy we use requires us to do some serious soul-searching. How can we say we love God and make energy choices that exhaust God's creation? How can we better practice "godliness with contentment" (1 Tim. 6:6)? What role should institutions—churches, schools, businesses, and governments—play in making a successful transition toward sustainable energy use?

Though the prospect of change may seem daunting, we can live by faith in God's promise: "If my people, who are called by my name, will humble themselves and pray and seek my face and turn from their wicked ways, then will I hear from heaven and will forgive their sin and will heal their land" (2 Chron. 7:14).

FOR REFLECTION AND DISCUSSION

1. What are some of the implications if, as predicted, worldwide oil production begins to decline in the near future? What responsibility or resources does the Christian community have for addressing the changes that will become necessary?

2. About 25-30 percent of the world's population lives entirely without the benefit of fossil fuels. What is our responsibility as Christians in the face of such unequal access to energy resources?

3. There is debate about whether or not global warming is a reality, and, if so, whether or not it is caused by human activities. Recount some of your personal experiences that suggest that the earth's climate is changing—not just temperature increases, but altered rainfall patterns and more extreme weather fluctuations too. If climate change is at least partly caused by human activities, how must we respond to this reality?

4. Some persons have suggested that one way to reduce demand for fossil fuels and to increase support for alternative energy would be to institute a substantial "carbon tax" on fossil fuels. The cost of this tax would be mainly offset by reduction of taxes in other areas so that the net tax burden on society would not increase substantially. Would you favor such a "carbon tax"? Why or why not?

5. In the face of declining availability of oil, we may one day need to limit our use of oil to "essential activities." Which activities would you deem to be essential, and which would you classify as non-essential? How might we decide on a set of activities that would be equally essential for all people?

FOR FURTHER READING

Deffeyes, Kenneth. *Beyond Oil*. Hill & Wang, 2005.

Goodstein, David. *Out of Gas*. Norton, 2004

Heinberg, Richard. *Powerdown*. New Society Publishers, 2004.

Meadows, Donella H., Jorgen Randers, Dennis L. Meadows. *Limits to Growth: The 30-Year Update*. Chelsea Green, 2004.

Roberts, Paul. *The End of Oil*. Houghton-Mifflin, 2004.

Simmons, Mathew. *Twilight in the Desert*. John Wiley & Sons, 2005.

RECOMMENDED WEBSITES

- The Oil Depletion Analysis Centre (ODAC) (http://www.odac-info.org/)

- U.S. Energy Information Agency (http://www.eia.doe.gov/).

- The Post Carbon Institute (http://www.postcarbon.org/).

- The Rocky Mountain Institute (http://www.rmi.org/)/.

- The BP Statistical Review of World Energy, 2005 (http://www.bp.com/genericsection.do?categoryId=92&contentId=7005893).

- Association for the Study of Peak Oil (http://www.peakoil.net).

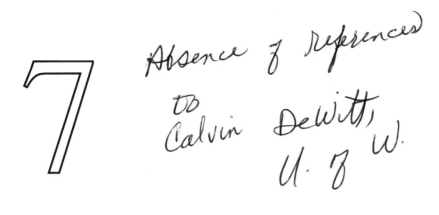

Absence of references to Calvin DeWitt, U. of W.

7

THE PLANTS WE GROW

DAVID R. CLEMENTS AND DAVID P. WARNERS

One spring, four-year-old Marcus Pin was helping his dad, Mike, in the garden. Mike was complaining about the weeds. Marcus asked, "Daddy, do you like weeds?" Mike answered, "No, I do not like weeds at all."

"Does Mommy like weeds?"

"No, Mommy doesn't like weeds either."

"Does Grandpa like weeds?"

"No, Grandpa doesn't like weeds."

"Does Grandma like weeds?"

"No. You should see Grandma's garden. There are never any weeds there."

Marcus paused a moment, and then asked the clincher: "Does God like weeds?"

A weed is usually defined as "a species out of place," so identifying an organism as a weed depends on the perspective of the gardener. To ecologists, weeds are more objectively understood as organisms with characteristics that allow them to thrive in areas where they are not native. Once free of the ecological balances that had kept them "in place," non-native species can increase unchecked. Many of our best-known weeds (including dandelions) originated in some other part of God's creation; their "proper place" is the area to which they are native (which, in the case of dandelions, is Europe).

Take a look at the plants growing in your garden or elsewhere in your neighborhood. How many of these do you think are actually native? A little research will show that very few garden and landscaping plants are native species. Take David Clements's neighborhood, for example. Dave lives in a subdivision in British Columbia called—rather ironically—"Forest Hills." It was created by removing the entire native forest and replacing it with a single tree species: the London plane tree, a native of Great Britain.

Inquiring about native plants at your local nursery will likely yield blank stares. That's because North American nurseries stock predominately European and Asian species. But does it really matter? What would be the best kinds of plants to grow in our yards and commons . . . and why?

Non-native invasive species spread and take over habitats. Some fear this is leading to the "homogenization" of creation. Author David Quammen warns that we are headed for a "planet of weeds," an increasingly uninteresting and ugly place in which to live. Do we really want every part of our world to look the same? Same birds (European starling); same trees (Norway maple); same plants (Kentucky bluegrass); same insects (the ubiquitous European cabbage butterfly)?

In Acts 17:26, the apostle Paul notes that God determines exactly where we are destined to live. The creation God requires us to help care for is a complex mosaic, diverse and knit together by mutually dependent relationships. Although modification of our landscapes is often necessary and expected, we are also called to recognize the inherent value of the land as it was formed by the Creator before people "remodeled" it.

God says, "If my people, who are called by my name, will humble themselves . . . then will I hear from heaven and will forgive their sin and will heal their land" (2 Chron. 7:14).

This suggests we must not see the land as merely a backdrop for the human drama of salvation, but instead develop a deeper reverence for the creation God dearly loves and desires to heal (see also John 3:16; Col. 1:15-20). How could such a commitment translate into our daily behavior in our own homes and communities? We'll focus on two issues where each of us can make a difference through our choices and actions.

INVASIVE SPECIES

Occasionally we hear sensational news reports of invaders among us, such as the recent report in British Columbia of an invasive bullfrog eating a kitten. The invasive coqui frog is making headlines in some areas of Hawaii because its 90-decibel "song" is making sleep difficult for residents and tourists. But these news stories are just the tip of the iceberg. Most alien invaders are far more clandestine.

Invasive species are sometimes referred to as "biological pollution." Unlike chemical pollution, which eventually degrades, biological pollution can proliferate indefinitely. Randy Westbrooks, an invasive species expert with the U.S. Geological Survey, has compared the need for greater awareness of invasive species to the concern over chemical pollution sparked by Rachel Carson's book *Silent Spring* in the 1960s. While he applauds the contribution of *Silent Spring,* Westbrooks feels today's public needs to recognize the more insidious and persistent threat of biological pollution.

Invasive species, the second leading cause of extinctions, are nearly as lethal as direct habitat destruction because they can fundamentally alter ecosystems. For example, invasive plants have changed the soil chemistry in many parts of Hawaii because they provide more nitrogen to the soil than native plants do, thus throwing the whole ecosystem out of balance. When invasive species replace native species, native plant interactions unravel. Still, you might ask, Isn't the movement of plants or animals from one part of the earth to another a *natural* process? True enough—except that the *rate* of movement is now many times faster, and incursions are much too frequent for natural processes to accommodate.

Some of these problems are so overwhelming that it's tempting to throw up our hands and "let nature take its course." But if we acknowledge our calling to serve and preserve God's creation (Gen. 2:15), then letting invasive species have their way is not a faithful response. In the words of Peter Illyn, head of Christians for Environmental Stewardship, "Extinction isn't stewardship."

Indeed, often we are slow to act. Our response is complicated by the fact that humans and nature have been interacting throughout history—the weeds are of our own making. In many cases, however, the appropriate response is clear, and there are opportunities for action. Invasive species councils are setting up "early warning systems" in many regions of the world, providing opportunities for volunteers to act as "informants." Volunteers are also being enlisted to remove invasive plants. By supporting such efforts, Christians can become tangibly engaged in promoting the welfare of the creation God loves.

RETURNING THE NATIVES

We believe in "the God of second chances." Indeed, redemption rings powerfully throughout the Bible, triumphing in the resurrection. In Joel's time, a massive invasion of locusts decimated the land, prompting the prophet to declare, "Surely the joy of mankind is withered away" (Joel 1:12). But in the very next chapter we read that restoration is God's ultimate vision for the land:

> Be not afraid, O land; be glad and rejoice. Surely the LORD has done great things. Be not afraid, O wild animals, for the open pastures are becoming green. The trees are bearing their fruit; the fig tree and the vine yield their riches. Be glad, O people of Zion, rejoice in the LORD your God. . . .

—Joel 2:21-23

We are called to join in God's restorative work as we live on this good earth. What better place to begin practicing restoration than in the part of creation that is our own backyard, however small? In their book *Caring for Creation in Your Own Backyard,* Loren and Mary Ruth Wilkinson make a number of practical suggestions:

- "dig deep down into the richness of life: plant a garden"
- "plant for the future with native tree species"
- "fight to preserve old trees and forests"
- "help wildness live on, sow seeds of local native flowers and shrubs."

Thinking about our yard more as part of God's creation and less as something we own ourselves is a good first step.

An appropriate next step is to ask, What can I do to help this part of the creation flourish? One approach is to re-establish natural relationships that were part of the land before it was developed. David Warners has dedicated much of the yard at his residence in Grand Rapids, Michigan, to a native species project. In the front, where it is sunnier, is a prairie planting. In the shady backyard are areas of woodland wildflowers, wetland vegetation, and natural groundcovers. The lawn that remains is managed organically and fertilized each fall with a top dressing of composted kitchen scraps and leaves.

The joy in having native plants is that they act as a magnet for other native creatures such as hummingbirds, goldfinches, butterflies, dragonflies, and moths. Furthermore, native plants do not require the chemical inputs that most non-native landscaping needs.

Using native plants in landscaping is just one small example of many restoration projects now underway. However, many people have probably never given the issue much thought. We tend to purchase alien plants for our gardens because they are often less costly and more familiar. Purchasing non-native plants is still an act of appreciation of creation, but choosing native plants in landscaping or restoring native habitats demonstrates a clear commitment to creation care; in so doing we can celebrate the very colors and textures God used to paint the our particular part of the creation mosaic.

We opened this chapter by saying that a weed is merely a plant out of place. But does "out of place" matter to God? What *does* God think about weeds, anyway? As disciples of the One who created the special places we live, we have a responsibility to take notice and respond when anything, including weeds, degrades the creation mosaic.

FOR REFLECTION AND DISCUSSION

1. Can you think of a particular plant or animal species that is native to the place you live? If you have difficulty with this question, does it bother you? How might you go about learning more about your local ecosystems?

2. Were you previously aware of the invasive species issue? Do you agree with Randy Westbrooks's contention that biological pollution is potentially more serious than chemical pollution?

3. Describe personal encounters you have had with weeds or invasive species. What negative and positive aspects did you experience?

4. Does the way we care for our own yards make a difference? Why? Native plant gardens are usually more "rough around the edges" than typical well-groomed gardens. How much should we be mindful of what the neighbors might think?

5. Composting is a good way to recycle kitchen and yard wastes without adding to landfills; however, if the compost is used before the decomposition process is completed, it can also spread weeds. Have you ever tried composting? Why or why not? Does your local village or city operate a municipal composting facility? Given the risk of weeds, do you think composting is good stewardship?

FOR FURTHER READING

Basney, Lionel. *An Earth-Careful Way of Life: Christian Stewardship and the Environmental Crisis*. InterVarsity Press, 1994.

Granberg-Michaelson, Wesley (ed.). *Tending the Garden: Essays on the Gospel and the Earth*. Eerdmans, 1987.

Shaw, Vera. *Thorns in the Garden Planet: Meditations on the Creator's Care*. Thomas Nelson Publishers, 1993.

Stein, Sarah. *Noah's Garden: Restoring the Ecology of Our Own Backyards*. Houghton Mifflin, 1995.

Wilkinson, Loren, and Mary Ruth Wilkinson. *Caring for Creation in Your Own Backyard*. Regent College, 1997.

THE WORK WE ARE CALLED TO DO

DAVID S. KOETJE

Ask most adults what their vocation is, and they'll probably tell you their occupation—what they do for a living. Ask them what gives them the most joy, and they'll likely mention something quite different—perhaps a hobby, a leisure activity, or some aspect of their family life. Certainly, recreational activities can be both sources of great personal joy and important elements of vocation. But they can also keep us from fully devoting ourselves to the pursuit of God's will.

In today's politically polarized and economically complex climate, we are tempted to put "the enjoyment of life" (Eccles. 8:15) ahead of God's call to justice (Amos 5:11-24; Micah 6:8). But the Bible is unequivocal about the connections between God's calling, our joy, and our neighbors' good. Furthermore, North American Christians increasingly recognize that the call to love God and one's neighbors (Luke 10:25-37) necessarily extends to our caring for creation (Rev. 11:18). Let's explore some of these interconnections.

"The place God calls you to," writes Christian apologist Frederick Buechner, "is the place where your deep gladness and the world's deep hunger meet" (*Wishful Thinking: A Seeker's ABC,* HarperSanFrancisco, 1993). Unlike the popular dualistic notion of vocation, in which what we do for a living merely provides the financial means to enjoy something else, this perspective points to a deeper level of meaning and joy in our work that is rooted in our discipleship. To know the place of our "deep gladness" requires a fair amount of personal reflection and meditation. And to know "the world's deep hunger" requires us to experience the world's pain, its dying to sin, and its resurrection to new life. If all this sounds a bit abstract, then perhaps a real-life example can provide some solid footing.

A ROCHA INTERNATIONAL

A Rocha (pronounced "a row´ sha"; "the rock" in Portuguese) is a Christian conservation organization dedicated to the care of God's creation in many places around the world. It is cross-cultural and community-based. One of A Rocha's conservation projects is unfolding in Surrey, British Columbia, at the Little Campbell River watershed. This watershed empties into Semiahmoo (Boundary) Bay along the Canada/United States border. The watershed and bay are vital to five species of Pacific salmon and hundreds of bird species.

A Rocha's presence at the watershed is no accident. Shortly after acquiring a 10-acre farm homestead from a Christian couple, codirectors Markku and Leah Kostamo identified multiple ways A Rocha could help conserve the watershed. Soon, teams of A Rocha volunteers, interns, and students from nearby Trinity Western University were working with the Little Campbell Watershed Society and Friends of Semiahmoo Bay Society to restore wildlife habitats in the watershed, plant trees along the estuary, and assist in community education. When the group started studying Coho salmon populations in the stream, the Semiahmoo Fish and Game Club, which operates a small salmon hatchery along the river, offered to help. And since farming is another component of this rural watershed, A Rocha has assisted local farmers in enhancing stewardship practices, focusing especially on those that affect stream quality.

Presently, the group is refurbishing a barn on the homestead to serve as a classroom, community center, and art gallery. A demonstration garden next to the barn promotes sustainable agriculture and serves as a "living classroom connecting people to land." Food from the garden may someday be served at a café inside the renovated Heritage Barn, where they hope to host community harvest festivals and ecological stewardship workshops. In all of these efforts, A Rocha promotes cooperation between local landowners, conservation groups, communities, governments, and the Semiahmoo First Nation (a native community).

A Rocha's work at the Little Campbell River watershed is just one example of what can happen when we respond joyfully to God's calling to be good stewards of the creation and good neighbors to all of its creatures.

CREATION-KEEPING

What does the Bible have to say about this notion of vocation? Consider Genesis 2:15: "The LORD God took the man and put him in the Garden of Eden to work (*abad*) it and take care of (*shamar*) it." Translations from Hebrew to English do not always do justice to this passage. Noting that *abad* is probably better translated as "serve," ecologist Calvin DeWitt surmises that "Adam and his descendents are expected to meet the needs of the garden so that it will persist and flourish" (*Earth-Wise: A Biblical Response to Environmental Issues,* Faith Alive Christian Resources, 1994).

This idea is the opposite of our usual notion that the creation is here to serve *us*—providing food, shelter, clothing, raw materials, and so on—although this too is a biblical theme. In effect, we are to serve creation as creation is to serve us. DeWitt notes that we participate in mutual "con-service," or conservation. Furthermore, the mandate of Genesis 2:15 calls us to *shamar* the earth. This same word is used in the Aaronic blessing "The LORD bless you and keep (*shamar*) you" (Num. 6:24). Our keeping mirrors God's keeping: God loves us, cares for us, and sustains us in our relationships to our natural and human environments, and we reciprocate by keeping creatures under our care in their proper natural contexts and providing them with God-given means to meet their daily needs.

Dominion is another important responsibility: "God blessed them and said to them, 'Be fruitful and increase in number; fill the earth and subdue (*kabash*) it. Rule (*radah*) over the fish of the sea and the birds of the air and over every living creature that moves on the ground'" (Gen. 1:28). The Hebrew words *kabash* and *radah* are very forceful. Do they give us license to exploit the earth?

To shed light on this question, the authors of *Earthkeeping in the '90s* (Eerdmans, 1991) reflect on another text in which God brings creatures to Adam to see what he would name them (Gen. 2:19). "The clear impression," they argue, "is that God *waits* for Adam's perception and for the creative (and responsive) act of his naming, as though it is in humanity that God's creation is made complete." Other Hebrew Scripture passages support this interpretation of dominion as a type of service to God and the creation. In fact, the prophets Ezekiel, Isaiah, Amos, and others often chastised Israel and Judah for inappropriately exercising dominion: abusing wealth and power by exploiting the poor and overworking the land.

A SENSE OF PLACE

What does this notion of Christian environmental vocation require of us? First, faithfully caring for creation requires us to develop a stronger sense of place. Place relates to the distinctive features of specific landscapes, habitats, and communities.

Fields, forests, deserts, and ponds are obviously unique places with distinctive features. Perhaps less obvious are the distinctive features of communities and farms in western Iowa or western Washington, southern Alberta or southern Ontario. Yet these similar places have different climates, soils, land forms, neighboring wildlife habitats, and even crops. These spawn rich nuances in farming practices, businesses, and community customs. Sadly, as we've seen in previous chapters, we tend to undervalue the individuality of places, and our inattentiveness to them erodes the very things that make these places special. Hence, a critical first step toward redeeming our fallen relationship with our lands and their inhabitants is attentiveness to the distinctive natural and cultural features of places.

2 Second, faithfully administering our calling requires us to serve these places. The term most often used to describe our caring for creation is "stewardship": management on behalf of a higher authority. Because a steward is subject to God, she cannot simply do as she pleases with creation. Furthermore, she cannot claim that stewardship only applies to certain areas of the Christian life, such as finances, and not to others. Stewardship applies to *all* our relationships within creation: land, water, and energy; ecosystems, habitats, and species; our places, our bodies, our work. Attentive stewardship promotes creation's well-being in all our endeavors.

As stewards we are called to honor God's covenant with the whole creation (Gen. 9:8-17) and to follow Jesus' example of dominion marked by servanthood (Phil. 2:5-8). As stewards, we need to ask ourselves some tough questions. Does our stewardship in the places where we live honor God's covenant? As Christ's disciples, do we serve the needs of our neighbors and our part of creation? Do we value the particular characteristics that make our places what they are?

We live in an age when distinctive ecological and cultural features of places are threatened by human activities. By simply going with the flow of our consumer culture, we contribute to this degradation of place. We need to recognize that our day-to-day lifestyle choices are spawning habitat fragmentation, pollution, climate change, and injustice. We need to recognize that these choices have consequences for our world: we import goods that could have been bought from local sources, while invasive pests and pathogens hop the globe in our cargo holds. And then we wonder why small local businesses go bankrupt and local habitats deteriorate. How can we claim to love the God who covenants with the whole creation while neglect-

who?

ing interrelationships that are key to the integrity of our places? Such a witness is hollow.

PLACE-BASED STEWARDSHIP

As we focus on the importance of interrelationships and our own embeddedness within creation, how then do we serve our places? Stewardship that is place-based has five essential characteristics:

- *Being attentive to the local ecology.* What species are native to the place, and what are their interrelationships? What interdependencies make these ecosystems resilient against forces that would threaten their integrity? What positive and negative effects do human actions have on this habitat?

- *Heeding the needs and knowledge of local communities.* What have we learned about our community's distinctive features and functions through our experience with it?

- *Letting local cultural values inform priorities and practices.* How do locally rooted values and experiences provide insights into appropriate stewardship?

- *Cultivating precaution, caring, and conservation.* How can we nurture the special features of the place? How can we encourage Sabbath rests and deter exploitation?

- *Collectively forging technologies, practices, and policies that enhance our embeddedness in places.* In what ways can we cooperate to enhance the interrelationships essential to the integrity of the place? How can we promote the flourishing of all its inhabitants, human and nonhuman?

These five characteristics are broad enough to encompass most of our occupations. They are also specific enough to help us evaluate our current stewardship practices, establish new priorities, and enhance our caring, keeping, and humble dominion of the earth. As Christian stewards, ours is a worthy and high calling of reconciliation and discipleship in the specific places God has put us!

→ He's got us giving the US to the native Americans.

67

FOR REFLECTION AND DISCUSSION

1. What are some sources of joy and deep gladness in your life? How do these relate to the place you live?

2. How does the example of A Rocha Canada's work in the Little Campbell River watershed demonstrate the difference place-based stewardship can make? What questions does it raise?

3. How has your sense of vocation developed over the years? How might adopting some of the elements of place-based stewardship further enhance your sense of vocation?

4. In what ways does your church or community struggle with its commitment to stewardship? How might the perspectives presented in this chapter help?

5. What would help you and your community to develop a stronger sense of place? How would this help you be more faithful stewards of your place?

FOR FURTHER READING

Basney, Lionel. *An Earth-Careful Way of Life: Christian Stewardship and the Environmental Crisis.* InterVarsity Press, 1994.

Bouma-Prediger, Steven. *For the Beauty of the Earth: A Christian Vision for Creation Care.* Baker Academic, 2001.

DeWitt, Calvin. *Earth-Wise: A Biblical Response to Environmental Issues.* Faith Alive Christian Resources, 1994.

"For the Health of the Nations: An Evangelical Call to Civic Responsibility." White paper, 9 September 2004, National Association of Evangelicals.

Harris, Peter. *Under the Bright Wings.* Regent College Publishing, 2000.

Plantinga, Jr., Cornelius. *Engaging God's World: A Reformed Vision of Faith, Learning, and Living.* Eerdmans, 2002.

Sider, Ronald J. *The Scandal of the Evangelical Conscience: Why Are Christians Living Just Like the Rest of the World?* Baker Books, 2005.

VanDyke, Fred, David C. Mahan, Joseph K. Sheldon, and Raymond H. Brand. *Redeeming Creation: The Biblical Basis for Environmental Stewardship.* InterVarsity Press, 1996.

Wilkinson, Loren (ed.). *Earthkeeping in the '90s: Stewardship of Creation.* Eerdmans, 1991.

RECOMMENDED WEBSITE

A Rocha International (http://en.arocha.org/home/). This website contains information about A Rocha's worldwide projects plus creation care articles, sermon/teaching guides, Bible studies, and other resources for Christian churches and groups.

WHAT WE DO FOR REST AND ENJOYMENT

PAUL HEINTZMAN

Every winter during my teenage and university years, I visited the home of Bill and Joyce Mason. Bill was a legendary Canadian filmmaker, canoeist, and artist. A typical visit to the Mason home in Quebec's Gatineau Hills would involve a church or university group engaging in a broomball or hockey game on the Masons' backyard rink, followed by a trail ski, followed by a hot meal and a viewing of one of Bill's already-popular or yet-to-be-completed films.

Bill cared deeply for creation, and was wildly enthusiastic about creation-based recreation. According to Ken Buck, Bill's filming assistant, that care for creation was rooted in Mason's Christian faith: "The single most power-ful compelling force behind Bill Mason's commitment to environmental responsibility was his deep unwavering Christian faith. Bill believed that man did not have 'dominion over' the natural world, but 'responsibility for' the natural world" (*Bill Mason: Wilderness Artist from Heart to Hand,* 2005). Bill hoped that sharing his joy of canoeing in films and books would encourage people to work for wilderness preservation "for the sake of all the myriad forms of life that live there. We have a responsibility to ensure that they continue to exist because they, like us, were created by God and have a right to exist" (*Song of the Paddle,* 1988).

RECREATION IN CREATION

When I visited the Masons' home in the 1980s, the professors in my recreation classes were teaching that by the year 2000 everyone would be working drastically fewer hours each week. Obviously, that hasn't happened. In a chapter called "The (Even More) Overworked American" (John de Graf, ed. *Take Back Your Time,* 2003), Juliet Schor documents how during the last 30 years North Americans have chosen increased working hours and an "orgy of consumption."

When our work and our recreation are characterized by consumption, we are using up rather than preserving and conserving creation's resources. Research shows that people who work less have less ecological impact (T. Kasser and K. W. Brown in *Take Back Your Time*). Furthermore, since most of us work indoors, only during our recreation do we have time to develop our awareness and knowledge of the created world. As the word *recreation* itself suggests, we can be *recreated* in the environment of *creation,* and during recreation we can care for and preserve creation.

But recreation can also be detrimental to creation, especially when it is technology-based and involves rebuilding creation to amuse ourselves with consumer goods. "We have become so totally committed to changing our environment," writes Mason, "that we have become oblivious to the fact that the world around us is a creation itself—God's creation" (*Path of the Paddle,* 1995).

SABBATH REST

As Christians, we need to ask ourselves about the impact of our recreation on creation. What do we do for rest and enjoyment? How do we forge a lifestyle of work and recreation that is respectful of creation? What place should recreation have in Christian discipleship?

Several biblical principles can help us understand the right relationship between recreation and creation. Let's start with the biblical concept of rest, which suggests that there is more to life than work. Biblical rest includes a range of physical and spiritual dimensions: a pleasant, secure, and blessed life in the land (Deut. 12:9-10); an entering into God's rest (Ps. 91:1); a rest of completion such as God enjoyed after creation (Gen. 2:2); a Sabbath rest of peace, joy, and well-being (Heb. 4:9-11); and a relief from labors and burdens as well as a peace and contentment of body, soul, and mind in Jesus (Matt. 11:28-30).

While we may not fully experience all these dimensions of rest until God's kingdom has fully come, we can begin to experience them now.

These elements of rest are part of the good life on God's good earth, and they provide insights into how we understand recreation. Of particular importance for our understanding is the Deuteronomic notion of rest in the land. As theologian Gordon Preece noted, "We don't rest in a doctrine, we need a place to put our feet up, but a place in which God is personally present" ("Re-Creation and Recreation in the Eighties," Conference of the AFES Fellowship). God's creation provides the context for our rest and recreation.

Like the biblical principle of rest, the Sabbath reminds us that there is more to life than work. In the creation account, the Sabbath points to a rhythm of work and non-work (Gen. 1-2). The same Sabbath rhythm is suggested in the account of God's provision of manna in the desert (Ex. 16), in the Mosaic law (Ex. 34:21; Lev. 23:1-3; Num. 28:18), and in the words of the prophets (Amos 8:5; Isa. 58:13-14). The Sabbath principle suggests that the rhythm of work and non-work, or recreation, is necessary for our well-being. Jesus demonstrated this rhythm in his life on earth. During his ministry, he regularly took time alone in the hills or solitary places to rest and pray (Mark 1:35; 6:31-32, 45).

Deuteronomy's version of the Sabbath commandment provides another reason why we are to stop working: "so that your manservant and maidservant may rest, as you do" (5:14). The Sabbath, therefore, is for human rest, restoration, and re-creation. It is "a day of sacred assembly" (Lev. 23:3)— that is, a day set aside for us to worship the One who created and sustains us. Jesus also taught that the Sabbath was a time for bringing healing and wholeness (Matt. 12:1-14; Mark 2:23-27; 3:1-5; Luke 6:1-4; 13:10-17; 14:1-6; John 9:1-41). However, in the Exodus account of the Sabbath commandment (20:8-11), we encounter the first reason God gives us for observing the Sabbath day: we should rest from our work just as God did after calling creation into being. The Sabbath was given not only for restorative purposes but also as a time to recognize that life is a gift from God and to respond with our worship and thanksgiving.

Exodus 20:11 suggests that observing a day of rest forcefully reminds us that we live in a world that contains all we need and many other things to enjoy. So the Sabbath is an invitation to experience the blessings of God's good gift of creation and delight in them.

Such delight in God's creation is evident in Bill Mason's feature film *Waterwalker.* Gazing at the wilderness around him, Mason says, "I look around me at the colors, the textures, the designs. It is like being in an art gallery. God is the artist. And he has given us the ability to enjoy all this, and to wonder, and in our own small way, to express ourselves in our own creativity, and that's why I like being here." Taken together, the Exodus and

Deuteronomy accounts of the Sabbath suggest that our recreation should be both for personal renewal and for appreciating and enjoying God's creation.

ENJOYING THE GOOD LIFE

The book of Ecclesiastes critiques those who distort God's intended rhythm of work and recreation by pursuing either a compulsive work ethic or a hedonistic recreation ethic based on consuming goods. The book points to an alternative for true disciples—enjoying the good life on the good earth God has given us. Throughout Ecclesiastes (2:17-26; 5:9-16; 6:7-9) and especially in 4:4-16, the author emphasizes the folly of compulsive work and refutes three arguments often put forward in its support: the need to achieve (4:4); the desire for wealth (4:8); and the desire to gain fame (4:13-16). The conclusion is unavoidable—overwork is foolish, and moderation is sensible.

In chapter 2, the writer of Ecclesiastes addresses those who hold a hedonistic, consumptive recreation ethic. A life of unreserved pleasure-seeking and acquisition of possessions is "meaningless, a chasing after the wind" (2:1-11). Evidently, recreation that is focused on pleasure-seeking, on consumption and acquisition, or that becomes one's all-consuming end, is ultimately not fulfilling.

The recommended lifestyle, in contrast, comes at the end of Ecclesiastes 2. Here we learn that life is to be enjoyed: "A man can do nothing better than to eat and drink and find satisfaction in his work" (2:24). Commentators suggest that this phrase stands for a contented and happy life characterized by joy, companionship, and satisfaction. The writer of Ecclesiastes further elaborates on the theme of enjoying the life God has given us (2:24-26; 3:12-13; 3:22; 5:18-19; 8:15; 9:7-9; 11:9-12:1). God has given humans the opportunity (and the encouragement) to enjoy the good life on God's good earth.

This advice to enjoy life reflects the Genesis account, in which God repeatedly pronounces the creation "good." It also reflects the rejoicing in creation suggested by the Exodus account of the Sabbath commandment, and the orthodox Israelite view of the earthly realm, in which God brings "forth food from earth: wine that gladdens the heart of man, oil to make his face shine, and bread that sustains his heart" (Ps. 104:14-15).

THE HEAVENS DECLARE . . .

Being good stewards of God's good creation implies that we should choose forms of recreation that help us to conserve rather than consume or exploit that creation. We've already seen how the Sabbath suggests that recreation is for personal renewal and enjoyment of creation, but it also suggests that our recreation should reflect care of creation. For example, both the Exodus and Deuteronomy versions of the Sabbath commandment (Ex. 20:10; Deut. 5:12-14) state that the Israelites' animals were not to work on the Sabbath; in fact, the Sabbath was also for the benefit of the animals: "Six days do your work, but on the seventh day do not work, so that your ox and your donkey may rest . . ." (Ex. 23:12).

Our recreation needs to respect, not exploit, God's creatures and the creation. That means we need to raise questions about "recreational" activities that use scarce energy resources and emit noxious fumes, such as auto racing or jet-skiing; or that abuse animals, such as bullfighting or hunting for "sport" rather than for food or other purposes. We need to question any recreational activity that needlessly upsets ecosystems or defaces natural beauty.

Instead we should choose forms of recreation that allow us to see, hear, and experience the majesty of God's creation. In *Path of the Paddle* Bill Mason talks about his visit to Banff National Park. By choosing to hike up Mount Rundle rather than take the gondola up Sulphur Mountain, he was able to experience that majesty firsthand. In the same book, Mason contrasts motorboat travel with canoe travel. He observes, "A journey by canoe along ancient waterways is a good way to rediscover our lost relationship with the natural world and the Creator who put it all together so long ago." Such recreation activities are consistent with the ancient tradition of meditating on creation—a form of contemplation that the mystics called the "discovery of God in his creatures" (see Ps. 8, 19).

In his film *Waterwalker,* Mason continues the tradition of contemplating the creation when he quotes Job 12:7-9:

"But ask the animals, and they will teach you,
or the birds of the air, and they will tell you;
or speak to the earth, and it will teach you,
or let the fish of the sea inform you.
Which of all these does not know
that the hand of the LORD has done this?"

All of this teaches us that recreation is part of God's lifestyle for us: for rest; for renewal; and for learning about, appreciating, and enjoying God's gift of creation.

FOR REFLECTION AND DISCUSSION

1. Before reading this chapter, what was your understanding of recreation? What new insights has this reading given you?

2. What biblical stories and personal experiences are especially helpful to you in gaining a healthier understanding of recreation?

3. What implications do the following have for your own recreation:

   • the biblical concept of rest?

   • the Sabbath commandment?

   • the book of Ecclesiastes?

4. Do you have a regular rhythm of work and recreation? If so, how has it affected your life? If not, what gets in the way of developing such a rhythm? Can you think of someone whose lifestyle models a healthy blend of work, recreation, and enjoyment of God's good earth? What can you learn from this person's life?

5. In what ways does your recreation help you learn more about creation, enjoy God's good creation, and care for creation?

FOR FURTHER READING

Buck, Ken. *Bill Mason: Wilderness Artist from Heart to Hand* (Rocky Mountain Books, 2005)

Heintzman, Paul. "Implications for Leisure from a Review of the Biblical Concepts of Sabbath and Rest." P. Heintzman, G.E. Van Andel, and T.L. Visker (eds.). *Christianity and Leisure: Issues in a Pluralistic Society,* 2nd ed. Dordt College Press, 2005.

Kasser T., and K.W. Brown. "On Time, Happiness, and Ecological Footprints." John de Graf (ed.). *Take Back Your Time.* Berrett-Koehler Publishers, 2003.

Mason, Bill. *Path of the Paddle*, rev. ed. Key Porter Books, 1995.

Mason, Bill. *Song of the Paddle*. Key Porter Books, 1988.

Schor, Juliet. "The (Even More) Overworked American." John de Graf (ed.). *Take Back Your Time*. Berrett-Koehler Publishers, 2003.

RECOMMENDED VIDEO AND WEBSITE:

- Bill Mason, *Waterwalker* (National Film Board of Canada, 1984).

- Go for Green. Active Living and Environment Program (www.goforgreen.ca).

10

SEEKING SHALOM

JOHN R. WOOD AND STEVEN C. BOUMA-PREDIGER

Close your eyes. Use your mind's eye to imagine a most peaceful setting.
Perhaps it's a majestic vista or a beautiful garden. Perhaps you are walking
along a forest path or quietly paddling a canoe. Or maybe you are sitting
down to a mouth-watering Thanksgiving meal with all your aunts, uncles,
and cousins. What do you see in your mind's eye? One of my most peaceful
early memories is sitting with my mom in church and listening to the
preacher while Mom tenderly rubbed my ear. This soothing gesture worked
to still the wiggles of a restless child on many a Sunday morning.

All of the peaceful images that may come to mind have something in
common—they are images of shalom. What is often missing in our visions
of peace, however, are the rest of God's creatures. We forget that God's
shalom extends to them as well.

THE VISION OF SHALOM

Shalom is a central theme of Scripture. From the first chapters of Genesis,
to the prophet Isaiah, to Luke's gospel, to the final chapters of Revelation,
we see that the kingdom of God is a reign of shalom—of peace and justice,
compassion and delight. And as the biblical texts vividly indicate, shalom
encompasses wolves and lambs, trees and soil, forests and rivers. It has to

do with all kinds of creatures—not only human creatures—living in right relationships. Shalom is as wide as creation itself. In his book *Not the Way It's Supposed to Be: A Breviary of Sin,* Neal Plantinga summarizes the expansiveness of shalom:

> The webbing together of God, humans, and all creation in justice, fulfillment, and delight is what the Hebrew prophets call shalom. We call it peace, but it means far more than mere peace of mind or a cease-fire between enemies. In the Bible shalom means universal flourishing, wholeness, and delight—a rich state of affairs in which natural needs are satisfied and natural gifts are fruitfully employed, a state of affairs that inspires joyful wonder as its Creator and Savior opens doors and welcomes the creatures in whom he delights. Shalom, in other words, is the way things ought to be (p. 10).

UNIVERSAL FLOURISHING

Shalom is "the way things ought to be," or God's will done on earth as it is in heaven. Shalom, in this view, is nothing less than the creation-wide realization of God's intentions for all things.

This vision of all things in right relationship is itself rooted in our understanding that God is a God of relationship. God is not solitary, not is God isolated or distant from creation. We humans are who we are only in relation—to God, to other people, and to the non-human world. We are embedded in a complex web of relationships that includes all creatures.

Throughout this book we have endeavored to keep in view this overarching truth: the God we worship—Father, Son, and Holy Spirit—is the Lord of all creation. God created all things in love, and that same God of love is making all things new through the redeeming work of Christ and the sanctifying power of the Holy Spirit. The shalom of God extends to the entire creation.

ACHING VISIONARIES

But at present everything is *not* the way it's supposed to be. God's good future has not yet come, for sin still has its way with us. Relationships are broken. People are alienated. The world groans for redemption. And so we ache for that time and that place when all will be set right, when what is misshapen is remade, when those who are estranged are reconciled. We ache for places of peace and communities of justice, for people of compassion and times of delight. As Nicholas Wolterstorff so poignantly reminds us, we Christians are "aching visionaries" yearning with all our being for God's good future of shalom.

What does that aching look like? What does this actually mean for how we live the good life on God's good earth? For the authors of this book it means we take seriously and joyfully the implications of our faith in all we do. It means we lean into that good future of shalom by asking some hard questions. And it means we act with creativity and courage to make real God's reign of shalom in our local communities.

We raised some of these hard questions in the previous chapters:

- How can our choices about the homes we live in bear witness to shalom? In deciding where and how to live, how can we better foster community and care for creation?

- How can our decisions about the food we eat contribute to God's shalom? How can we decrease our support for CAFOs while increasing our involvement in the local farmer's market? *confined animal feeding operations*

- How can our choices about the clothes we wear give evidence of our allegiance to God's kingdom of shalom? What can we do to avoid supporting sweatshops?

- How can our decisions about the energy we use help bring about shalom? In what ways can we curtail our use of fossil fuels and pursue renewable energy sources?

- How can our choices about our yards and community commons make for shalom? What can we do to eradicate invasive species and cultivate native plants in our own backyard, in the school playground, in the county park?

- How can our decisions about the work we are called to do testify to God's good future of shalom? How can we come to know more intimately our local place?

- How can our choices regarding rest and recreation bear witness to shalom? In what ways can we properly honor the Sabbath and choose forms of recreation that conserve rather than consume God's creation?

- What, in sum, does it mean to seek shalom in the practices and activities of our everyday lives?

BOTH GIFT AND TASK

This earth is God's world of wonders. It is a place filled with hope and promise by the God who crafted it, sustains it, and lovingly works to redeem it. We have not been left alone to struggle in confusion. Rather, we are a body of believers, each of us called to love God and to serve each other and all that God has made. This is our joyful vocation—to love God; to care for that which God loves; and to seek shalom—the flourishing of all things. That is the vision we seek by God's grace to live out as we live the good life on God's good earth.

In her insightful book on Sabbath, Marva Dawn writes that if "we learn to pray to be a people of shalom, then throughout the week we will seek to spread that peace throughout the world" (*Keeping the Sabbath Wholly*). Shalom, in other words, is both gift and task—something to be gratefully received from God and something to be sought after and worked for.

May we be aching visionaries who yearn for God's good future of shalom to be realized in our world. And may each of us be empowered by the Holy Spirit to bear witness to that shalom in all we do.

FOR REFLECTION AND DISCUSSION

1. In a sentence or two, sum up what shalom means to you. What might it look like in your everyday life?

2. What does caring for creation have to do with shalom? How have you experienced shalom with the rest of creation?

3. Chapter 2 suggests that we make shalom, rather than profit, the guiding principle of our lives and work, with the goal of living sustainably and at peace with the creation. What are some societal issues—as opposed to personal issues—that prevent us from achieving shalom?

4. According to Marva Dawn, "On Sundays we learn [by praying together] to be a people of shalom." Write a prayer for shalom based on a theme in one of these chapters.

5. What are three ways that you and your community can seek shalom?

FOR FURTHER READING

Dawn, Marva. *Keeping the Sabbath Wholly: Ceasing, Resting, Embracing, Feasting*. Eerdmans, 1989.

Johnson, Darrell. *Experiencing the Trinity*. Regent College Publishing, 2002.

Plantinga, Jr., Cornelius. *Not the Way It's Supposed to Be: A Breviary of Sin*. Eerdmans, 1995.

Wolterstorff, Nicholas. *Lament for a Son*. Eerdmans, 1987.

Wolsterstorff, Nicholas. *Until Justice and Peace Embrace*. Eerdmans, 1983.